VINTAGE

FOR THE LOVE OF ART

Sajitha Madathil is a theatre and film actor, writer and feminist activist. She is one of the founding members of the drama troupe Abhinetri and of the Women in Cinema Collective. She is the recipient of several awards, including the Kerala State Film Award (for *Shutter*, 2012), the Kerala Sahitya Akademi Award for Drama (*Arangile Matsyagandhikal*, 2019) and the Kerala Sangeetha Nataka Akademi Award (*Malayala Nataka Sthree Charithram*, 2010). In 2020, she received the Kerala Sangeetha Nataka Akademi Award for contributions to drama. Her publications include *M.K. Kamalam* (2010), *Aranginte Vakabhedangal* (2013), *Neelakkuyil: Miss Kumariyude Chalachitrajeevitham* (2020) and a memoir, *Vellivelichavum Veyilnaalangalum* (2025).

Jayasree Kalathil is the author of *The Sackclothman* and has translated seven books from Malayalam to English. Her translations have won the Crossword Book Jury Award (twice), the JCB Prize for Literature, the V. Abdulla Memorial Translation Award and the Mathrubhumi Book of the Year award. She was also shortlisted for the American Literary Translators Association's National Translation Award in Prose.

ADVANCE PRAISE FOR THE BOOK

'*For the Love of Art* is a fascinating and radical intervention in cultural history that transforms the story of theatre in Kerala, not only by filling gaps and remedying omissions but also by consciously rewriting it with women at the centre as subjects and agents. Sajitha Madathil's absorbing narrative, in this wonderful English translation by Jayasree Kalathil, reads a wide-ranging array of resources—much of it new—with the astute perceptiveness of a feminist artist–activist–scholar, turning the passionate glint in the eyes of the artists who appear in these pages into the "star–sparkle in the annals of forgetfulness". The significance of this book, which hardly has any precedent, goes beyond Kerala to open up fresh avenues for critical feminist historiography in India'—**Udaya Kumar, former professor, Jawaharlal Nehru University**

'As an actor, I found Sajitha Madathil's history of women in Malayalam theatre immensely useful in understanding the complex fabric of our social structure, from which women actors emerged to follow their dreams. In Jayasree Kalathil's translation, *For the Love of Art* is a powerful testament to the courage and tenacity of women in the acting profession who battled—and continue to battle—for their rights'—**Revathi, actor and director**

'Sajitha Madathil's *For the Love of Art* is a compelling work that unearths the forgotten histories of women in Kerala's theatre. With great eloquence, Madathil weaves together lives, stories and performance histories to create a tapestry that is both poignant and urgent. This book, in Jayasree Kalathil's English translation, is a most welcome addition to theatre scholarship. It will be of interest to practitioners and theorists alike, for it is as much a powerful story of perseverance and love—which is what has kept women's theatre practice alive at all—as it is about the nitty-gritty of theatre-making itself'—**Anuradha Kapur, teacher and theatre practitioner**

OTHER BOOKS IN THE CHRONICLES SERIES

Courtesy of Criticism: Selected Essays of Kirtinath Kurtkoti (edited and translated from the Kannada by Kamalakar Bhat)

My Truth: Autobiography of Narmadashankar Dave (translated from the Gujarati by Abhijit Kothari)

A Glimpse of My Life: Autobiography of Ram Prasad 'Bismil' (translated from the Hindi by Awadhesh Tripathi)

Being Modern: A Biography of Ananda Ram Dhekial Phookan by Gunabhiram Barua (translated from the Assamese by Banani Chakravarty)

For the Love of Art

The Lost History of Women in Kerala Theatre

Sajitha Madathil

Translated from the Malayalam by
Jayasree Kalathil

VINTAGE

An imprint of Penguin Random House

VINTAGE

Vintage is an imprint of the Penguin Random House group of companies whose addresses can be found at global.penguinrandomhouse.com

Published by Penguin Random House India Pvt. Ltd
4th Floor, Capital Tower 1, MG Road,
Gurugram 122 002, Haryana, India

First published in Vintage by Penguin Random House India 2025

Copyright © Sajitha Madathil 2025
English translation copyright © Jayasree Kalathil 2025

All rights reserved

10 9 8 7 6 5 4 3 2 1

The views and opinions expressed in this book are the author's own and the facts are as reported by her which have been verified to the extent possible, and the publishers are not in any way liable for the same.

Please note that no part of this book may be used or reproduced in any manner for the purpose of training artificial intelligence technologies or systems.

ISBN 9780143468042

Typeset in Adobe Caslon Pro by MAP Systems, Bengaluru, India
Printed and bound in India by Replika Press Pvt. Ltd.

This book is sold subject to the condition that it shall not, by way of trade or otherwise, be lent, resold, hired out or otherwise circulated without the publisher's prior consent in any form of binding or cover other than that in which it is published and without a similar condition including this condition being imposed on the subsequent purchaser.

www.penguin.co.in

Contents

Author's Note: Writing Women into History ... ix
Translator's Note ... xxiii

1. Out of the Shadows, Gently: Women and the Birth of Theatre in Kerala ... 1
2. Rivalling Real Women: Female Impersonation in Tamil and Malayalam Musical Dramas ... 10
3. Into the Limelight: Early Heroines of Musical and Social Theatre ... 19
4. Making a New Malayali Woman: Women's Agenda in the Theatre ... 62
5. On the Political Stage: Women in the Leftist Revolutionary Theatre ... 89
6. A Balancing Act: The Theatre as Workplace ... 135
7. Into the World of Contemporary Malayalam Theatre ... 188
8. Of Her Own: The Emergence of Women's Theatre ... 203

References ... 223
Notes ... 231

Author's Note

Writing Women into History

In 2002, I had written and acted in a mono-play titled *Matsyagandhi* ('She Who Has the Fragrance of Fish'). A well-known theatre director came to know of this, and told me, 'you are a good actor. So why are you trying to do this writing job that is not yours?'

In the theatre world of Kerala, there were relatively fewer women who did the unwomanly job of writing plays or dared to author the texts they performed. For a long time, women's participation in theatre was based on this division of labour: Men write and direct; women act. As women, you perform what is authored by men. If you want to express autonomous agency, it can only be through the meta-text you create out of the text and the roles created by male authors.

The written history of this world, in most cases, has also been dominated by male icons, individuals who authored the texts, directed them and starred in them. Why were women's contributions left out of these histories? Writing the history of Malayalam drama literature, G. Sankara

Pillai said that his intention was not to present Malayalam dramatists and their works in chronological order, but to refer to important works and playwrights who have 'become beacons because of their talent', and to specifically examine trends that have developed over time.[1] That no women or their works figured in considerations of important works, talented dramatists or specific trends is significant. It is quite possible that women's works were fewer in number because they did not have the confidence to publish or perform their works given their lack of access to the technical aspects of playwrighting and production. Still, it is curious that even well-known works such as Kutti Kunju Thankachi's *Ajnathavasam*, Lalithambika Antharjanam's *Savithri, Adhava Vidhavavivaham*, B. Saraswathiyamma's *Devadoothi* or Madhavikutty's *Madhavivarma* find no mention in these histories.

Women, then, are rarely present as natural subjects of theatre history writing. But despite this marginalization, women's role and involvement in Malayalam theatre cannot be ignored. They hold a central position in theatre practice in terms of labour, economics and entertainment; their presence, although anomalous and contradictory, is important. Sources, often fragmented, exist attesting to their involvement and contribution in the broader field of cultural production.

Earlier histories have left out even the names of women who were, although in smaller numbers, a significant part of theatre, and what was recorded often was careless. For instance, anyone who investigates women's involvement in the early years of the theatre will find in most of the famous history texts a reference to a play titled *Subhadradhananjayam* written by Thottakkattu Madhaviyamma. This record, faithfully repeated by attentive historians in subsequent texts, is in fact a reference to *Subhadrarjunam*, written by Thottakkattu Ikkavamma, a well-known poet and dramatist of the time, and the mother of Thottakkattu Madhaviyamma. Histories written after the 1980s include women and their contributions albeit as a subsection on sthree natakavedi—women's theatre—and not as a part of mainstream history. Often, these are incomplete descriptions of our contributions to theatre post-eighties.

I am a part of the theatre-culture, whose legacy I bear in practice and scholarship, and this book happened because of my intervention as an activist and academic in the Kerala theatre space. The histories I trace here through a feminist historiography are also an act of claiming my own legacy—a female legacy.

When, towards the end of the nineteenth century, Malayalam theatre began to take shape, were women active in Kerala's public sphere? This was one of the first questions I wanted to explore. The cultural space at the time had women-centred and women-led games, dances and songs. Drama emerged in the 1890s not so much as a continuation of this rich culture, but almost as a new art form. Its secular nature was different from community art forms. Women found it hard to enter this space despite it being one where people from diverse social strata and hierarchy came together to work. And yet, to my surprise, I found women playwrights writing dramas that were well received. Thottakkattu Ikkavamma and the women before her such as Kutti Kunju Thankachi wrote dramas at a time when women were living in a society that controlled their every movement and behaviour. In Chapter 1, I trace the sociocultural context around the space of the theatre and the gendered and caste-based moral codes that governed women and their appearance in the public sphere.

While trying to track information about a former generation of women actors, I found that even casual mentions of their names were few and far between. Meanwhile, details about 'female impersonators'—men who played female characters—have been recorded meticulously. During an interview for a magazine, the conversation I had with Mavelikkara Ponnamma, a former actor who shared the stage with female impersonators, helped me understand the phenomenon of female impersonation and how it had determined the methods and mores of 'acting female'. I also began to realize that the disturbing male gaze that women actors still encounter today was experienced by men who performed women characters on stage, and this gaze, steeped in the views and mores of the society and its male desires, shaped their body language. Mavelikkara Ponnamma told me about her experience of performing the role of Vasavadatta in the play, *Karuna*, a role performed to great appreciation by Ochira Veluktty, the most famous of all female impersonators in Malayalam theatre: 'I became him, the great Velukkutty . . . and then I became Vasavadatta . . .' To play the role, she studied his body language as he performed on stage rather than her own female body because the audience expected a specific rendition of womanhood on stage that 'rivalled real women', a phenomenon I discuss in Chapter 2. I explore the trajectory of acting techniques of female impersonation in theatre from Kerala's traditional and classical art forms to the current theatre practices. By the early twentieth century, women began to step bravely on to the stage of sangeetha natakam—musical dramas. In Chapter 3, I look at their interventions in this space even as ideas about womanhood and 'female acting' continued to be influenced by body language, movement and appearance consolidated by female impersonators.

In 1994, with two other women theatre students—C.V. Sudhi and S. Sreeletha—I founded a women's theatre group called Abhinethri. We produced a play, *Chirakadiyochakal* ('Sounds of Flapping Wings'), planning every aspect of it ourselves without any outside intervention. It was a huge challenge within the patriarchal space of Kerala's theatre, but we managed and performed the play successfully all over Kerala. The media considered it to be 'the first women's theatre group'. We were pleased about our achievement. It was only later that I discovered that women had come together and produced plays before too. The play, *Thozhil Kendrathilekku* ('To the Workplace') was written during the Namboothiri reform movement by women of the Antharjana Samajam, a collective of women from the Malayala Brahmin Namboothiri community, in 1948, and it was performed by an all-women cast in nine centres. Learning about this play, ignored by theatre historians, took me by surprise. I began reading the play and it was like recovering an archival resource which could intervene into larger narratives. Another play that was forgotten and retrieved later by feminist writers was the unpublished text of *Savithri, Adhava Vidhavavivaham* ('Savithri, or Widow Remarriage', 1938) by the famous Malayalam writer Lalithambika Antharjanam. Discussions about the forgotten history of these two plays and their subsequent retrieval in theatre led me to analyse the historical context of drama as part of the Namboothiri reform movement, which is discussed in Chapter 4. The movement had at its heart a keen interest in addressing 'the woman question', and the Yogakshema plays of the 1920s and 1930s voiced the clarion call for improving the community's backwardness by highlighting the dreadful conditions under which its women lived. These plays introduced women characters who raised and addressed critical questions pertaining to their existence. Detailed readings of these plays demonstrate how male writers of the movement created famous women characters in the plays and how these affected real women in the social arena.

However, the lives lived by the heroines of the reformation movement were far more dramatic than the characters represented in these plays. Women playwrights of the time were more connected to the perspectives of women reformers who were their contemporaries. Even in the plays authored by male leaders of the reformation, women characters appear mostly in the kitchen or domestic spaces, while women playwrights imagined characters with agency, who speak out about social issues and appear in spaces outside the kitchen such as libraries and living rooms. Overall, the famous male-written plays of the Namboothiri reformation, advocated the continuing preservation of the domestic sphere, now endowed with a modernity that was somewhat restricted, while continuing to deny women autonomous agency. These works clearly show the first generation of gendered consciousness in the Namboothiri community.

I met actors M.K. Kamalam and Seethalakshmi two decades ago. In my long conversations with them, their creative lives were revealed in all their complexity. They talked about why they reached out into the public space as actors and why the Kerala social reform movement's agenda for women was limited. By the time these conversations took place, they were in their late seventies, and their memories of many personal events were not as clear. However, their memories of the theatre were still sharp and powerful. They were not in great physical health, and sometimes needed help to walk, but they asked me for the chance to get a role in a play or a film. Passion for acting never dies, I realized after meeting them. Most of the women actors of the social and political theatre of the early twentieth century were from marginalized communities. The theatre drew women into the public arena, but the limited nature of its agenda for women sent them back into the domestic sphere. In Chapter 5, I present the life stories of some of the women actors of political theatre, including those I had the good fortune to meet and talk with. An analysis of the relationship between the early twentieth-century public sphere in Kerala, which was shaped by the mechanisms of caste and patriarchy, and the lives of actors, who managed this space at these intersections, needed the addition of the crucial category of gender. How did creative women artists manage to pursue a profession in theatre acting? What kind of resistance did they confront from casteist, patriarchal and hierarchical orders that ruled the public sphere and how did they deal with it throughout their lives? It seemed to me that women characters in political plays, the women artists playing those roles, and the women activists involved in political work had little in common. As a social activist, I was already aware that women represented as incapable of agential action in political dramas were miles away from the women within the political movements the plays were portraying. I also discovered that an actor's life story complicates and strengthens concepts of the public and private as well as femininity and masculinity. It was also fascinating to consider how the family as an institution contributed to constructing a challenging lived experience for these women actors.

My life in theatre, television and film has allowed me to meet the heroines who shaped political theatre. I got to interview K.P. Sulochana as part of the *Penmalayalam* programme, a documentary about women in Kerala broadcast on Kairali TV that I produced and presented. By the time I met her, she had almost stopped participating in her theatre group. She was mostly earning an income by travelling to Gulf countries with her music group. Consumed by health issues, she was finding it challenging to pursue singing, but her unstable financial situation did not allow her to take time off to rest even in her sixties. I was also involved in making a short documentary about K. Devayani, a Left-wing social activist. Diving into the life struggles of these women led me to finding out more about their contemporaries including performer-activists from that period.

The lengthy conversations I had with P.K. Medini and Nilambur Ayisha helped me understand the intricacies of the lives of women cultural activists. I produced a long documentary on the life of P.K. Medini in 2011. I also wrote the preface to Nilambur Ayisha's autobiography, *Jeevithathinte Arangu* ('The Stage that is Life'). These interventions helped me look at political plays through the eyes of these women and their artistic careers that were seldom talked about at that time. Naturally, the question of how women in political plays were confined to the four walls of the home while, in real-life politics, women like Devayani were participating actively came up. The political and cultural life of women like P.K. Medini and Ayisha gave rise to conflicts in their social identity. For them, art was life and not just a financial resource. Women actors in political dramas and their contributions were overlooked or not given room in mainstream theatre history writing initiatives until the feminist reconsideration of this period. Re-reading Kerala's political drama texts and its gendered politics as well as revisiting the past as remembered by women performer-activists provide a strong critique of the feudal and colonial power structures and gendered social relations still existing in the public sphere of theatre.

In Chapter 6, these discussions are taken forward by looking at the theatre as a workplace where women were entering in much larger numbers. In the Malayalam theatre scene, it is in the professional theatre that most women are employed. I explore the circumstances that brought these women into the theatre world, and how both the stage and the society perceive them. Does this workplace provide them with the basic rights that all women should have at their workplaces? How do they negotiate the particular rigours of this workplace that demand time away from home and family, long trips on the road, irregular working hours and income and so on? I had many conversations, some in-person interviews and others using a long questionnaire, with women working in this space, including some of the important personalities in theatre such as Savithri Sreedharan, Kuttyedathi Vilasini, Shanthadevi, Vijayakumari, Beatrice, Stella and Elsie Sukumaran. Some of them had to leave the theatre due to personal circumstances. Memories of their days in the theatre, on stage, in drama troupes made them bloom with happiness even as they worried whether they would ever be able to return to the stage. The life of a full-time woman theatre professional is filled with much more diversity compared to their counter parts in the amateur scene, yet history does not deem it necessary to document this.

By the 1980s, and with a feminist movement and women's organizing firmly in place, women's involvement in theatre also began to change. Chapters 7 and 8 explore the lives, experiences and contributions of a new generation of women who began to take an active interest in theatre. Armed with professional training as well as training through participation in women's and street theatre, they began to participate in amateur and professional theatre and set up women's collectives and drama groups. I, too, am a part of this generation of women actors. I have acquainted myself with Kerala's social and creative life from the 1980s as an artist and with the insight gained from my engagement with feminist and political activities, which helped me dive deeper into the history of theatre in Kerala. Writing the original Malayalam version of this book, *Malayala Nataka Sthree Charithram* (The History of Women in Malayalam Theatre), in 2010, was not an accident. It was a conscious act of writing women actors into theatre history that had silenced, sidelined and shunned them. Women-centred approaches that developed in the 1980s with women's interventions in history writing, media and other activities have formed the basis for writing this book. I drew inspiration and insight from historian and translator J. Devika's scholarship on the social life of Malayali women and Tracy C. Davis's studies on histories of theatre.

In the early days of doing this work, one day I was talking to a famous director about my interest in studying the lives of women in professional theatre. 'What is there to study about them?' he asked, a sentiment I then encountered several times expressed by several people. Then I spoke to a woman actor who began telling me her story. 'Only seventh-class educated I am, but I always wanted to be a stage actor. I did a few amateur plays and then, for years, I was part of the professional theatre.' As she told me this, her eyes sparkled. History had hidden this star-sparkle in the annals of forgetfulness. But it stayed with me along with the insights she gave me into the lives of women like her.

This book is a deep personal engagement with theatre practice and critical historiography. Such endeavours are only the beginning to deconstruct canonical histories of theatre practice in Kerala. I hope it offers critical questions and methodological approaches to revisit critical sites. My primary aim in writing this book was simple—to write a history of theatre in Kerala that included the experiences of women as theatre workers. It does not offer up a systematic and linear account of women artists in theatre. Instead, it attempts to explore and connect, through myriad and meandering paths, the stories of women within the theatre space in Kerala.

When Jayasree Kalathil approached me with the proposal to translate this book into English, I was pleasantly surprised. I wondered whether readers outside Kerala would understand the contexts and conflicts of women's lives within its theatre space. I had written many of the instances and events with Malayali readers with an understanding of the contexts in mind. In the process of translating, Jayasree spent a considerable amount of time delving deeper into these, to unearth their meanings and emphasis. And in that process, the book has gained richness and detail, and wiped away my anxieties about it being translated by someone unconnected to the world of theatre. Our many conversations in the last year have enriched each stage of the translation and given me immense pleasure. I am grateful to her for choosing to translate this book when she was invited to be part of Chronicles, the series of non-fiction translations undertaken by the Ashoka Centre for Translation and Penguin Random House India, thus giving a wider platform for the marginalized history of women theatre workers in Kerala.

There are, no doubt, many facets and experiences, and many more stories of women artists, that have been left out. So I do not see this history as a definitive one, but as the beginning of many such works to come. Already, in the years between the original publication in 2010, and its translation now, there have been a handful of academic theses and essay collections published on this subject. I hope there will be many more in-depth works in the future.

Sajitha Madathil

Translator's Note

When I was invited to translate a book for Chronicles, a non-fiction project, I was excited but also somewhat doubtful. I like translating fiction and poetry and had not translated much non-fiction other than a few essays and campaign material. A whole non-fiction book seemed daunting. But which book? I wanted the book to be significant, genuinely engaging with a social-cultural or political question in relation to Kerala. I wanted it to be of interest to a range of readers in the way it was written. So, I consulted several of my friends—historians, cultural theorists, fellow writers and translators—and they suggested several texts, among which was one that recurred several times: Sajitha Madathil's *Malayala Nataka Sthree Charithram*. I contacted Sajitha and she sent me the text. I read it and found an interesting, straightforward history of women's engagement in theatre in Kerala, written from an insider's perspective.

As with most cultural histories, histories of theatre in Kerala routinely left out women from its narratives about drama as a literary form and as performance art, giving barely any space for the roles, experiences, engagements and contributions of women within it. Rather than attempting to fill these gaps in traditional history writing, Sajitha tells this story by placing women firmly at its centre as rightful creators and owners of its cultural capital. Here we find stories about a whole range of women, their contributions, struggles and triumphs, spanning a period starting with the latter half of the nineteenth century to the beginning of the twenty-first. Unnamed women who were part of folk theatre and traditional arts; dramatists who were never fully acknowledged as authors; actors who were required to follow ideas of femininity established within the parameters of the male gaze and the phenomenon of 'female impersonation'—men performing female roles; actors who turned activists through their participation in political dramas; actor-workers who were forced to spend decades earning their livelihood in the cesspit of exploitative theatre; academicians trained in drama as an artform; feminists who worked to create a women's theatre. We meet and learn about the lives of many women who came into this field, who excelled, burned out, disappeared, survived. In the process, we learn about the gendered nature of Kerala's theatre.

However, it is not only its gendered analysis that makes this book special. It is the fact that it places drama and theatre as part of a public sphere of social and political activity marked by notions of caste, class and community, and that it brings in elements that may, at first glance, seem outside the realm of writing the history of an artform. Sajitha records the history of social, cultural and political developments in Kerala theatre, including the early links with Tamil musical drama traditions, the influence of social reformation, the freedom struggle, the growth of a communist ideology, the origins and activities of theatre groups and art collectives such as the Kerala People's Arts Club (KPAC), connections with other performance arts and film, the development and current status of professional theatre and so on. And she does this without ever losing sight of the lives of the women involved in it, their hopes and aspirations, their psyche, their very body and its functions.

What touched me deeply when I read this book and later when I delved deeper into it as the translator is also the act of naming that Sajitha undertakes. Throughout the text are analyses, stories and anecdotes that make women present, visible, *named*, acknowledging, finally, their rights to intellect, culture and art.

The original book, which won the Kerala Sangeetha Nataka Akademi Award, was published in 2010. Translating this book was also an opportunity to refresh the book. Sajitha reread each chapter, and we had many discussions based on which we reorganized some chapters and added new material and background where relevant.

I am grateful to Sajitha for patiently answering all my queries—as an outsider to the field, there were many—and for chasing references and details, and making the process of translating this book a genuine pleasure. My thanks also to Sunandan K.N., Bindu Menon and Karunakaran for answering my questions about historical events, and for the discussions on how to translate certain phrases and ideas; to the Ashoka Centre for Translation and Arunava Sinha for inviting me to be part of this project; and to Vineet

Gill and Saloni Mital at Penguin Random House India for editing this book with a fine eye for detail. Once again, I am convinced that translation is a collaborative project.

Jayasree Kalathil

1

Out of the Shadows, Gently: Women and the Birth of Theatre in Kerala

'Naari nadichidam nasham bhavichidam.'

'Damned is the place where a woman is acting on stage.' This proverb captures the attitude of Malayali society towards women who enter spaces of self-expression in terms of acting. In the nineteenth century and through to the mid-twentieth century, as Malayalam theatre took shape, this proverb and the sentiments it captures continued to be prevalent in Kerala.

Writing the history of women in Kerala theatre requires an understanding of the contexts and complexities of the lives of women at the time when the space of the theatre was consolidated. Did the circumstances then allow women access into the public sphere as writers, actors and directors? Were they able to assert the freedom of body and mind that performing on public stage required? As we attempt to answer these questions, we find that towards the end of the nineteenth century, the participation of Malayali women in theatre was determined by their social circumstances and bodily autonomy.

Rigid ideas about honour and dignity that existed in Kerala in the nineteenth century were largely predicated on women and the unwritten rules that governed every aspect of their lives.[1] These rules dictated how women from different caste-communities were to behave. Several proscriptions existed around menstruation and reproduction, as well as prohibitions such as not having contact with men other than their husbands; not travelling outside of the home in the night; not leaving their hair loose and untied; what not to wear; and so on.

Social norms prescribed how women from different castes were to dress. For instance, women from the Ezhava caste (classified currently as OBC—Other Backward Caste) were not allowed to wear a mundu that reached below their knees. The privilege of covering their knees with a mundu that was wider—the acchipudava as it was called—was reserved for upper-caste women including Nair women. Only the antharjanam—'the folk inside', as women from the Malayala Brahmin Namboothiri caste are referred to—had the right to cover their breasts. Women from all other Hindu castes were denied this right. In the nineteenth century, a major outcry broke out when a few women from the Channar community who had converted to Christianity began covering their breasts with an upper cloth or a rowka (an early version of the blouse) or both. Disgruntled upper-caste men unleashed a volley of violence against any woman who dared to cover her breasts. The events that followed, the fight for the right to cover their breasts, led especially by women from Dalit communities, or the Channar Lahala (revolt) as it came to be known, marks a key moment in the history of Kerala.[2]

By the beginning of the twentieth century, the feeling that it was shameful that women were required to leave their breasts uncovered in public was widespread. And yet, as recorded by Padmanabha Menon in his history of the state of Kochi, Sir Ramavarma Maharaja, then ruler of the realm, proclaimed that Nair women had to remove their upper garments if they wished to enter temples for worship.[3]

Women had to endure severe, violent punishments if they disobeyed these rules. Several descriptions of such punishments exist in historical records. Bhaskaranunni describes one such incident: 'A Channar woman who walked along a lane in Kayamkulam with a piece of cloth across her chest was caught by some savarna men. They snatched away the cloth and hung the tops of baby coconuts (vallakkamodu) from her nipples.'[4] A souvenir of the golden jubilee of the SNDP Yogam records another incident: 'We have heard that a skirmish had broken out when a group of angry Nair men had attacked and forced an Ezhava woman to remove her mundu because it had covered her knees.'[5]

The Diwan of Thiruvithamkoor, T. Madhava Rao (known widely as Diwan Madhavarayar) released an order prohibiting women from the lower castes from imitating upper-caste women who had the right to cover their breasts. This prompted a public reply from the governor of Madras, Sir Charles Trevelyan, questioning and criticizing the order. In his autobiography, the former chief minister of Thiruvithamkoor-Kochi, C. Kesavan, recalls this incident thus:

> The reply, in short, emphasized that the royal powers in Thiruvithamkoor would do well to remember that the ruler of the British empire was a woman, and that she would not stand aside and watch while the womanhood of her sisters was being denigrated. It also contained a threat that, if need be, the issue would be resolved at the sharp end of a bayonet ... A royal decree followed that allowed women to wear whatever they wanted ... Rejoicing in this freedom granted to women, one of my female ancestors distributed neryathu (a long cloth to cover the upper part of the body) to several women from the Ezhava community.[6]

The prohibition on wearing a rowka continued for quite some time after. One of the arguments used to rationalize this prohibition was that the rowka was not Keraleeyam—part of the culture of Kerala—and that it was like the kuppayam, the wearing of which denoted religious conversion into Islam. Wearing a rowka and an upper cloth was seen as performance, as disrespect towards elders. C. Kesavan describes an incident when the journalist and social reformer C.V. Kunhiraman's wife was scolded by her mother-in-law for wearing a rowka. 'Take it off right now! Where do you think you're going dressed in a kuppayam like an aattakkari, an ummachi!' Here, the terms 'aattakkari' (dancing girl) and 'ummachi' (Muslim woman) are both clearly being used as slur.[7]

It is against this social background that Malayalam theatre takes shape. While several such restrictions existed on clothes, behaviour, access to public space and so on, there also existed performing arts—both folk and classical—that allowed for visual representations of creativity. However, for the modern Malayali woman emerging at the end of the nineteenth century, these spaces rapidly became inaccessible, while the new forms of stage arts failed to provide alternatives. Yet, women excelled in language, literature and the classics even when denied access to education as we define it today, and there are several descriptions of their knowledge and artistry. For instance, C.V. Kunhiraman, journalist and founder of the newspaper *Kerala Kaumudi*, writes about a young woman who had taught him to read and interpret the Ramayana when he was a boy, and her unique ability to read the text in several different ragas. Elsewhere he writes about a valyammavi, an elder aunt, born at the beginning of the nineteenth century, and her scholarship: ' . . . there is a misunderstanding that school education began in recent times, especially when it comes to women from the Ezhava community. My valyammavi is an example that proves otherwise. Until she lost her eyesight, it was her habit to read the Ramayana in the evening for several hours into the darkness.'[8]

Women's subjectivities during the emergence of Malayalam theatre, then, were governed by a complex social situation that both allowed and restricted their participation in writing plays and performing on stage. Their activities within the field need to be studied with this social milieu in mind. Many women from the upper social strata were allowed education as long as it took place within the private space of the home. Two such women were Kutti Kunju Thankachi and Thottakkattu Ikkavamma. Although the history of Malayalam theatre barely mentions them, they were among the early playwrights who, despite not knowing much about the dramatic art, wrote critically-acclaimed plays based purely on their creative abilities.

Early Women's Writing in Theatre

Historical records credit Kutti Kunju Thankachi (1820–1904) as the first woman to write a play in Malayalam. Thankachi's real name was Lakshmikutty, and her early education was under her father, Valiya Irayimman Thampi, who taught her Malayalam, Tamil, debate and grammar. Thankachi became famous as the composer of three aattakkatha—music for Kathakali, a specific genre of poetry in Malayalam. She also wrote several poetic compositions in the form of traditional songs such as Kaikottikkali song, Oonjal song, Kurathy song, and popular songs about the god Sreekrishnan and about temples. Her play, *Ajnathavasam* (Life Incognito), written in Kollavarsham 1066 (1890 CE), took inspiration from the Sanskrit plays of the time.[9] *Ajnathavasam* dealt with the episode from the Mahabharata of the Pandavas' exile in the forest followed by a year of living in obscurity without being recognized. In his history of Kerala literature, the poet Ulloor S. Parameswara Iyer adjudged that Thankachi's play had turned out to be something that could be read and enjoyed by literary aficionados, and that it was 'an adequate accomplishment with some dimly sparkling jewels of inspiration scattered within it'.[10] Despite the fact that she was an established writer, as well known as others who wrote plays during the time, Thankachi's work did not become part of the established history of Malayalam theatre.

Following in Thankachi's footsteps was Thottakkattu Ikkavamma (1864–1916), who wrote the play, *Subhadrarjunam*.[11] Ulloor refers to it as deserving of a place within the central oeuvre of Malayalam plays: 'Only the epic poets Kodungallore Thampurakkal have written such plays before this, an exception being Kutti Kunju Thankachi's *Ajnathavasam*. *Subhadrarjunam* is the second of the plays written by women and was published at the end of Kollavarsham 1066 (1891 CE).'[12]

Thottakkattu Ikkavamma firmly believed that women had as much right as men to engage in and nurture literature, and that anyone with a determined mind could enchant appreciators of the literary arts. However, there were those who suggested that the works attributed to Ikkavamma were written by the dramatist Chathukutty Mannadiyar. The literary magazine *Vidyavinodini* came to her defence, saying that 'the writer was deserving of being called Thunchath Ezhuthachan of the female gender'.[13] Readers of *Subhadrarjunam* will have no doubts about Ikkavamma's knowledge and ability in the technical aspects of writing plays. The text is testimony to a seasoned hand and contains precise instructions for stage placements, movements and acting.

The play was contemporarily translated into Sanskrit by renowned scholar Karamana Keshava Sasthri. Attesting to the attention it received are the several articles that appeared in literary magazines and newspapers of the time. Ikkavamma was influenced by the changes taking place in playwrighting as well as stage performances, and was fully involved, more than was usually possible for women at the time, in the field. At the very beginning of the play, the soothradharan (storyteller/narrator) proclaims: 'It is only men of substance who can fulfil the dharma of poetry. I don't believe that a woman's involvement in this can ever be good enough.' To which a female character replies: 'It is my belief that a woman can successfully undertake any task that a man can.'[14]

There is plenty of evidence to show that women in this period were influenced by artists, performances and appreciation of drama. It was during this period that Kerala began to become familiar with theatre in Tamil, especially the Tamil sangeetha natakam or musical drama. In 1892, when T.C. Achuthamenon wrote *Sangeetha Naishadham*, it immediately sold over 34,000 copies. 'In composing this work, he was instigated and encouraged by his maternal aunt, Ikkavamma of Thrissur Ramanchira Matam,' writes Ulloor in his history of Kerala literature. 'It seems Ikkavamma had watched the Manomohanam Company perform *Abhijnana Shakunthalam* (by Keralavarma Valiya Koyithampuran) and had invited them to Thrissur. This performance was heavily influenced by Tamil theatre, but the musical content, as a matter of fact, was too little. She then requested her nephew to compose a play that was different from this, and that, in effect, was what sowed the seed for *Sangeetha Naishadham*.'[15]

When *Sangeetha Naishadham* was performed for the first time in 1892, Achuthamenon performed one of the roles (that of the Kattalan) and Ambadi Govinda Menon enacted the role of Damayanthi. Ikkavamma too took to the stage, performing as Nalan, one of the central characters.[16] Theatre history credits 'Ikkavamma of Thrissur Ramanchira Matam' as the first woman to act in a Malayalam drama. But why didn't she perform the female role of Damayanthi, opting, instead, to play Nalan? Did she choose to play this part because it was the most important? Or would she have chosen the male part as a ruse to camouflage her female body in the public sphere? In any case, the history of theatre marched on, from Ikkavamma who hid her female body within a male character to the world of male actors who played female roles in musical dramas. In other words, women made their entry on to the stage by providing a new language of performance to an important chapter in the history of Malayalam theatre, that of the Malayala sangeetha natakam, the musical theatre in Malayalam.

2

Rivalling Real Women: Female Impersonation in Tamil and Malayalam Musical Dramas

In the 1880s and 1890s, when Kutti Kunju Thankachi and Thottakkattu Ikkavamma were writing plays in Malayalam, women were actively participating in Tamil theatre next door. While male actors in Malayalam theatre embraced fame as female impersonators, playing female roles on stage, histories of Tamil sangeetha natakam tells us stories of Tamil women setting up their own theatre groups and excelling on the stage playing male parts.

One such sangeetha natakam company, headed by a woman named Balamani Ammaiyar, who would become famous as Kumbakonam Balamani in the annals of history, travelled across Tamil Nadu, set up camps in different places and put up performances. In Malayalam theatre, as Ikkavamma of Ramanchira Matam enacted the role of Nalan and hid her performing female body within the male character, Tamil female bodies were, although in a strictly controlled way, enthralling an adoring audience, stimulating sexual desire and making financial profits. One play in particular, titled *Tara Sasankam*, increased the company's earnings substantially. *Tara Sasankam* was not only a hit wherever it was performed; it also instigated debates.[1] In the play, a goddess named Tara is cursed to take human birth as a queen. In one scene, a naked Tara is seen applying oil on the naked body of her lover, Chandran. The characters, both depicted by women actors, wore tight, skin-toned clothes in order to allow the audience to imagine that they were naked. In my interview with the famous theatre artist and activist Mangai, she recalled how generations of actors who came after talked about this incident. People surged in to watch the play wherever it was performed. In Kumbakonam, a special train named, appropriately, 'Balamani Express' was put into service to ferry people from all over the region to the venue of the performance.

Whan Balamani and her troupe visited Thiruvananthapuram, a large crowd gathered to watch them. Pleased with their performance, the then minister of Thiruvithamkoor presented her with a gold chain, putting it around her neck in full view of the public. The incident took place in 1903 and paved the way for serious and humorous discussions. One of the early proponents of freedom of press in Kerala, 'Swadeshabhimani' K. Ramakrishna Pillai, wrote about the incident: 'O, Travancore state! The predicament you have reached! You who were governed by noble ministers with high ideals who evoked fear and wonder among the inhabitants of neighbouring states, we cannot understand what sin you have done to be trapped now under the misgovernment of a wicked minister taken in by female charms.'[2] This comment, from one of the period's most progressive thinkers, attests to how Kerala viewed a woman actor and her creative abilities.

So what was happening in Malayalam theatre as the Balamani Express whistled its way through the towns and villages of Tamil Nadu? How did Tamil culture influence our theatre? Tamil drama sets first began to perform in Thiruvananthapuram between 1865 and 1870. This visual feast made its entry into the milieu of folk dramas and other indigenous visual art forms that the Malayali was familiar with, bringing with it elements that the ordinary theatre-goer found pleasurable. Its particular features included music and women performing female roles on stage. Sthreepart was the term used to describe all female roles, including that of the lead, in drama. While in Marathi and Parsi theatre, men acted in sthreepart, in Tamil theatre, men and women took on these roles on stage. Tamil women actors such as K. Sundarambal, S.D. Subbalakshmi, Krishnaveni, Sarada and others were actively involved on stage alongside famous 'female impersonators' including Brahmasri Ananthanarayana Iyer and Kutteeswaran.[3]

Beginning in the 1890s, Malayala sangeetha natakam flourished as a branch of the theatre until around 1955. However, despite the example of pioneering women such as Ikkavamma of Ramanchira Matam, social circumstances still prevented women from taking to the stage as actors. Perhaps this was why, up until the 1920s, female roles on the Malayalam stage were played mainly by men. Men impersonating women was not uncommon in Malayali cultural spaces; female impersonators were a routine and large part of visual art forms such as Kathakali—arguably the best-known form of dance drama—as well as the ritual art Mudiyettu, and folk drama forms such as Porattu, Kannyarkali and Kakkasseri Natakam. This tradition continued into the new art form of drama. Moreover, male actors who routinely enacted female roles were an integral part of the stage in other states in India too. Jai Shankar Sundari (1889–1975) on the Gujarati stage and Bala Gandharva (1888–1967) on the Marathi stage were well-known female impersonators. Malayala sangeetha natakam followed in this tradition.

All histories of male actors who played female parts in Malayala sangeetha natakam must begin with Ochira Shivaprasad Velukkutty (1905–1954). An incredible phenomenon in the history of Malayalam theatre, Ochira Velukkutty's contribution to the theatre, in a life that spanned barely fifty years, is timeless. In the preface to his biography of the actor, K. Sreekumar writes that this 'female impersonator' possessed a feminine beauty on stage that rivalled that of 'real women'.[4]

Ochira Velukkutty excelled in representing female characters in a space that was inaccessible to women. And just as women actors have been, by and large, forgotten in histories of the theatre, he too was sidelined. After having worked actively for over forty years in the field, his death, at the age of forty-nine, went unnoticed by most of his colleagues. Throughout his career, he was lauded for his creative talents in the theatre world, even as he was embroiled in various altercations in his personal life and within his own drama company. Could this have been because he was meted out the same second-class treatment that was reserved for those who played sthreepart? He, too, was subjected to the same taunting, lustful gaze that women artists were subjected to, and continue to experience, within the field. 'Many were the times when fans rushed into the greenroom, aroused by Velukkutty in his female garb,' writes K. Sreekumar in his biography of the actor. 'As numerous were the occasions when peeping toms turned their lustful eyes on his beauty through the holes in the coconut-palm walls of the greenroom.'[5]

The biography makes note of several incidents where Velukkutty had to subject himself to physical examination to convince sex-crazed fans that he was indeed a man: 'Once, during a performance of *Karuna* (an adaptation of Kumaranasan's poetic masterpiece of the same name), Velukkutty had stepped outside, still in costume as the heroine Vasavadatta, to urinate. Assuming that he was a woman, a gang of hooligans grabbed him and forced him into a jeep. "I'm a man," he screamed, but they did not let him go until they had conducted a physical examination.'[6] And at a performance in Alappuzha, 'Velukkutty came on stage in his costume as Vasavadatta. A section of the audience began arguing that this was not a man in woman's costume but a real woman, and insisted that they would not let the play begin until a physical examination was conducted. Helpless, Velukkutty had to let himself be examined.'[7]

In fact, these humiliating incidents were not aimed at Velukkutty the actor, but the femininity he embodied. Given this societal context, women were reluctant to come forward as stage performers. Sebastian Kunjukunju Bhagavathar (1901–1985) was a renowned actor, playwright who wrote musicals and social dramas; a drama company owner, and one of the most influential personas in Malayalam theatre. In his memoir that encompasses theatre history and remembrances of his colleagues, Bhagavathar recalls the situation where men played female characters on stage:

> Those were the days when women had not yet accessed the stage. How the Master [V.S. Andrews, who was his stage guru] would train the men who played female parts! I salute those memories with folded hands still. We were put to shame and sat with our heads bowed every time the handsome, dignified master of the craft transformed through gestures and expressions into a beautiful, young woman right in front of our eyes.[8]

V.S. Andrews (1872–1968) played an important part in popularizing theatre, wrote and directed plays, and trained a considerable number of theatre actors. Bhagavathar's recollection of how he directed his plays makes clear that it was the director who defined the expressions and movements of female characters and conveyed those to the male actor who played these roles through directorial input. Elsewhere in his memoirs, we can read how the actor impersonating a woman acted out these ideas. 'The audience in those days found it exhilarating to watch Velukkutty and me on stage together,' writes Bhagavathar. 'Their enthusiastic appreciation of Velukkutty's depiction of feminine modesty and bashfulness, more realistically portrayed than a real woman would have, and my enacting of masculine majesty were indications of how the world of theatre recognized our talents.'9

What we see then is how the actor Ochira Velukkutty, who enacted female roles with 'feminine modesty and bashfulness more realistically than a real woman', becomes the personification of the male-defined language of the performance of femininity on stage. Modesty and bashfulness become values and imperatives of femininity, a language that is defined and constructed by men, and becomes the reality of womanhood on stage. However, it is not on stage alone that a play fulfils its meaning. The gender, caste, class and communal nature of the audience play a significant part in how stage performances are interpreted.

It is also evident that Ochira Velukkutty's female characters and the characteristics of femininity that they ensconced have influenced women actors who came after him. Prominent among early women actors was Mavelikkara Kamalam, who had shared the stage as a supporting actress with Ochira Velukkutty in the plays *Karuna* and *Thilothama*. Sebastian Kunjukunju Bhagavathar recalls her acting prowess in his memoirs:

> At one point, Velukkutty left the stage for a year and went off to Hrishikesh as a sanyasi. During this time, at a performance of *Karuna*, led by Kuzhiyil Nanupillah, who was the manager, Sreemathi Kamalam performed the role of Vasavadatta opposite Ochira Sankarankutty Nair as the hero. It is a memorable fact that she was able to satisfy the audience through a performance that emulated Velukkutty in each gesture and expression.

Velukkutty came back after a period and resumed his role, and Kamalam continued serving as the supporting actress in the role of Vasavadatta's maid.[10]

At the height of Velukkutty's fame as female impersonator, the audience as well as the theatre expected and readied women actors to emulate the movements, stage presence, gestures, costume and make-up that he had institutionalized. The image of the woman that emerged from the efforts of playwrights, directors and male actors playing female roles, and the ideas of womanhood, held by women newly entering the space as well as those fostered in theatre-goers who had grown accustomed to performances of femininity by male actors like Velukkutty, combined to form a new bodily language for women. How women actors of the time reconciled with this new language is to be found in their own words.

One of the most famous women stage actors of this period was Seethalakshmi, who had acted alongside Velukkutty in a noteworthy role in the play *Karuna*. I interviewed her as part of the research for this book. Referring to Velukkutty as 'the epitome of womanhood', she recalled: 'Faced with the beauty of his female impersonation, even real women would admit failure. There was not a single female actor capable enough to challenge his prowess in female roles. I consider it my utmost fortune that I had the opportunity to act beside him as a maid in the play. There has never been an actor, before or since Velukkutty, who could perform the role of Vasavadatta as brilliantly as he did.'

Seethalakshmi was a prolific actor and had opportunities to act alongside such doyens as Palluruthi Lakshmi and

Mavelikkara Ponnamma, and yet, in her estimation, Velukkutty's female impersonation holds pride of place.

Mavelikkara Ponnamma herself had high praise and reverence for Velukkutty. In an interview with Muralidharan Nair, she talked about a letter Velukkutty wrote to her requesting her to stand in for him at a performance. 'I am so weak that I can barely stand up,' he told her. 'Please perform my Vasavadatta. You can do it. And I will consider it a great help if you do.' Ponnamma recalls how this request put her in a quandary.

> I thought to myself, I would perform any play in the world, but not *Karuna*. Velukkutty was what made the play. No one aware of his performance as Vasavadatta would even consider playing that role. I was in a dilemma. So, I went to him to take his blessing before the performance. Reaching out from his bed, he stroked me. By God, how will I ever forget that! I had his blessing. Even my voice changed.[11]

What ensued was a tactical interpretation whereby the woman actor borrowed from the master's craft as well as from the ideas of womanhood that she herself held, giving form to a new language of the stage, which enthralled the Malayali audiences who were admirers of the performances of doyens such as Velukkutty. This was a mode of acting that did not question the audience but emerged from seeking to satisfy their expectations. This situation complicated the entry of women on to the stage. As time progressed, women would enter this space in larger numbers and claim their rightful place through their own talents.

3

Into the Limelight: Early Heroines of Musical and Social Theatre

In his memoir, *Natakasmaranakal* (Memories of the Theatre), Sebastian Kunjukunju Bhagavathar narrates in detail the story of how one of the early woman actors of Malayalam drama, Palluruthy Lakshmi, entered the theatre in the early 1930s:

> One day, while we were searching for an actress to stand in for Velukkutty for the heroine's role, we were approached by Kochanjeri Narayanan, a percussionist who played the mridangam. He said, 'Sir, I heard that you are looking for an actress for the heroine's role in your drama? There is a woman named Lakshmi in my place. She is a music teacher at our school, and she sings well. She often takes part in concerts as well, and I play the mridangam for her performances. If you'll allow, I'll bring her to you.' We were overjoyed and agreed on a date before he left. We were astonished that a woman was ready to step on to the stage on her own volition

when it wasn't a common occurrence. Anyway, we didn't bother to search further for an actress until we met with her.

On the decided-upon day, the man showed up at our camp in Aluva by one o'clock with a woman as he had promised. We judged her at a glance. The young woman was very beautiful and elegant. She had a few books, an umbrella and a lunchbox with her as she was on her way to school, and had come to us with Narayanan without informing her husband or her family.

The next morning, I woke up, and when I went to the riverbank to bathe as usual, four policemen approached me. 'Sir, we heard there is a drama camp set up in Aluva,' they said. 'Is that the building they are in?'

'Yes,' I said, 'What do you want?'

'We received a complaint that a man named Kochanjeri Narayanan came to the drama camp with a woman named Lakshmi,' they said. 'We are here because of this petition filed at the Palluruthy police station by the woman's husband and parents. Do you know anything about this, sir?'

'Yes, that man and woman did come to our camp,' I said without trying to hide anything. 'They haven't woken up yet. Please wait here, I'll come with you after I have my bath.'

After my bath, I led them to the camp. I explained the situation to our tutor Swami Brahmavrathan and our music teacher, Ochira Raman Bhagavathar. Mr Francis, the owner of our company, had gone home. The petition asked that Lakshmi present herself at the police station. I told the policemen that I will see to it, but they demanded to see Narayanan and Lakshmi. They were frightened when they heard of the policemen's visit. 'Don't be scared,' I said, 'I will immediately inform the company owner and we will go to the police station as soon as possible.' I also wrote a letter agreeing to take them both to the inspector and sent the policemen back.

After they left, I coached Lakshmi how to answer the questions the inspector might ask and lifted her spirits. By this time, Mr Francis arrived. He was a rich and influential man. We got ready to leave for Palluruthy. Raman Bhagavathar, Swami, Mr Francis and I escorted Narayanan and Lakshmi.

The petitioners were already there when we arrived. When Mr Francis introduced us to the inspector, he asked us to sit. He read the petition. 'Is it true that this man, Kochanjeri Narayanan, abducted you as it says here?' he asked.

'No,' Lakshmi said. 'I went to Aluva of my own volition. I asked him to accompany me because I knew my husband and parents wouldn't permit me to go to Aluva. He plays mridangam at my concerts. My husband doesn't even approve of my giving concerts. I knew he wouldn't let me join a drama company if I were to tell him. My husband has always been a barrier to my dream of being self-reliant by honing my God-given skills and earning my own money. I'm requesting you to terminate our marriage. I am responsible and ready to take care of my parents in their old age according to my capability.'

'Did you hear what she said?' The inspector asked Lakshmi's husband.

'Yes,' he replied.

'So, are you ready to divorce her?'

After thinking for a while, he nodded in agreement.

'Alright, then. Both of you must write the agreement and sign it.'

Thus, their marriage was terminated.

Then the inspector spoke to Lakshmi. 'Let's move on to the next step. Lakshmi, you are joining a drama company on your own. A woman has never stepped into the Malayalam drama industry till date. You deserve all the praise for opening a new door for the talented women of our land. But there is one thing you should consider. It would be rather difficult and sometimes even dangerous for a lone woman to be a part of a party full of men, and that too, a drama party. There will be different types of people in the company and living with them might be a struggle. So, it will be better to begin your journey in drama after you choose a life partner who appreciates and encourages your talent and skills.'

These words from the knowledgeable and art-loving inspector were very important. All of us agreed that he was right in his opinion too.

'Would you like to accept Narayanan, the man who encouraged you to take this opportunity, as your lawfully wedded husband?' asked the inspector.

It was as though the doctor had prescribed exactly what the patient had wished for. She said 'yes' in a low voice. When the inspector urged her to give a clear answer, she said she would love to do so.

Their marriage was registered almost immediately in the presence of Lakshmi's parents and the rest of us.

Thus, Lakshmi and Narayanan became a wedded couple. This marriage was peculiar for a few reasons. Firstly, it was a deed done by registering an agreement which was a very rare occurrence in those days. Secondly, it was an inter-caste marriage which was frowned upon by almost all communities. Thirdly, it was a matrimonial union primarily for advancement in art. For all these reasons, their marriage attracted a lot of attention, and brought more fame and recognition for our art committee.[1]

Bhagavathar thought it important to record the occasion in such dramatic detail. In addition to marking an important milestone, the excerpt is replete with anecdotes about the social hardships a woman was confronted with if she chose to work in the field of drama, including dealing with society's censure that women who stepped out of their homes could not survive without the support of men. There is very little information about early women actors of Malayalam music dramas; their presence is rarely found even in historical texts on Malayalam drama. Yet, their presence was significant to the development and trajectories of theatre in Kerala.

It was in the 1930s that women began to occupy the space of the theatre in considerable numbers. The sociopolitical changes in women's situation, taking place all across in India, paved the way for the opening up of this space too. Western, colonial culture, ideas and ideology began to spread through English education, setting off clarion calls for changing the inequalities in social and legal spheres, including caste reform, equal rights for women, arguments against child marriage, widow remarriage, and so on. Raja Ram Mohan Roy (1772–1833), Ishwar Chandra Vidyasagar (1820–1891) and others played key parts in challenging these ideologies steeped in male dominance that controlled the lives of women in Bengal during colonial times.

Social reform in twentieth-century Kerala was spearheaded by reformers such as Sree Narayana Guru, Chattampi Swamikal, Ayyankali, Vagbhatanandan, Vakkom Abdul Khader Moulavi, Poykayil Appachan and so on. Reformation movements led by these social reformers gave rise to a new social consciousness in Kerala, with the question of gender taking centre stage. By the 1920s, these clearly voiced discussions began to leave visible marks in the public sphere. A large percentage of the women who began to view theatre as their workplace were from communities that were marginalized in terms of economics and caste.

Discussions about women's position in society were quite common in the Kerala public sphere at the time. By the 1920s, the first generation of Kerala women who had had modern education were already coming forth to demand basic civil rights, including job reservations, right to vote, legislative representation and so on. Simultaneously, writings by women on general matters concerning women were published in various magazines, many of them under the editorship of women. The general thrust of these discussions was that all women shared certain characteristics and interests and that these were essential for building a modern society. J. Devika, in an article about the early writings of Malayali women, observes that even when women were making their own money and living independently, they were expected to relay signs of self-control, interest in domesticity and maternal instincts.[2] L. Meenakshikutty Amma, in an article initially published in the *Mahilamandiram* magazine, explains the primary position of women and why it is important for them to work:

> Is it possible for only men to work in order to protect and nurture themselves as well as the majority of women? . . . Among the communities with lower education and reform statuses and higher poverty, women too go to work with men for daily wages. Even though the particular duty of women is to take care of their household matters, the same cannot be said in terms of severely poor population . . . Among the well-off families, it's the man's duty to work and earn while the woman has to take care of the household. Still, even the most strict and thorough housewives find extra time on their hands after a day's work . . . To be able to help their hardworking husbands to tackle financial issues by putting their own effort and being independent is a prideful achievement for these housewives.

She adds that women who do not have enough educational qualifications could always take up sewing and weaving from their homes to make extra money.[3]

Understanding the lives of women actors in this period in history is important in terms of their changing roles in the newly emerging spaces in theatre as well as in society. They shared a common space and the experience of the gendered dichotomy with women who were in public spaces while also tasked with reinforcing moral standards of domesticity. Many of them learnt music and trained in drama as children in Bala Natana Sabhas (schools for aspiring young actors) and went on to perform on stage, all the while being under the supervision of their fathers or brothers. Several of them also went on to act in films. Marriage came along while they were riding the wave of success in the world of theatre and, in several cases, put an end to their artistic lives. Several of them were hounded by attitudes and actual acts of violence that stemmed from moral judgements that cast women in public spaces as 'available women' with loose sexual mores, 'harlots'.

The entry of women into the public sphere was becoming more possible, but they were not able to enjoy this space to the fullest. While they were pleased with the financial rewards and popularity it brought, they did not enjoy full freedom. The money they made from their career was often controlled by their fathers or other male family members. And when they got married and the control of their lives transferred to their husbands, they had to give up acting. Most available documents about women actors of this era contain lines to this effect: 'Retired from the scene after marriage and led a quiet life'. Their interviews attest to the fact that they continued to live on bearing the uneasiness of being parted from their passion.

Janaki Srinivasan argues that social reform movements promoted a new modern patriarchy constituted by enlightened domesticity and complementarity between the sexes.[4] Education, maternal health and fertility control were in service of equipping women to fit into idealized gender roles for the sake of the family, community and nation. And because of this, employment in non-feminine professions and political participation remained low.[5]

Many of the early women actors in sangeetha natakam theatre were those who had trained in Bala Natana Sabhas and went on to shine in 'mahal sets' (the main or major set that includes all the important and well-known actors and singers; there would also be a minor set with less important actors and singers). During their training, they had opportunities to learn about trends in Tamil and Parsi musical theatre as well as Malayala sangeetha natakam that was undergoing rigorous growth at the time. While social reform movements brought these women into the public sphere, as soon as they were married, their creative ambitions died a suffocating death within their family lives, steeped to this day, in male dominance. Most of these women stopped performing as soon as they were married. Still, a rare handful remained, holding on to their art until the end of their lives.

The first challenge one faces when trying to explore the life narratives of these early women actors in the workplace of the theatre is that the record of this history is spotty and sporadic with no dedicated archive. In writing this chapter, therefore, I have depended on hitherto untold stories derived from my interviews with some of these women, their writings and memoirs, information from archives, as well as existing scholarship. In order to analyze the status of women in 1930s Malayalam theatre, their creative lives as artists need to be documented first, and the manner in which they negotiated the early twentieth century public sphere in Kerala which was structured through the modalities of caste and patriarchy, and its intersection with gender.

In his memoir, Sebastian Kunjukunju Bhagavathar writes that, although he had never met her in person, he had heard that Varkala Ammukkutty was the first 'professional woman actor' of the Malayalam stage. 'Women were routinely seen on the Tamil stage, which seems to have finally pricked the conscience of our caste-proud society,' he writes, commenting on her presence on stage. 'The artistic fervour deep within women's hearts seems to have finally woken up.'[6] A document and photograph is available attesting that Varkala Ammukkutty had acted in the drama *Vyazhavattathinu Shesham*, performed by Sree Chithira Thirunal Granthasala. Following in her footsteps came others such as Palluruthy Lakshmi (life period unavailable), Seethalakshmi (1919–2009), C.K. Rajam (1920–1995) and M.K. Kamalam (1923–2010). In exploring their stories, I try to answer these questions: What kind of resistance did women actors have to face from caste and patriarchal orders that governed the public sphere? How did they face up to these challenges?

Women's education in Kerala at this time focused on training in music, modern languages, fine needlecrafts and painting. Early women actors in Kerala were skilful and trained in music, and they considered theatre acting as a source of income generation. Once the Malayalam music drama became a new workplace and many interested women came forth to be a part of it, these women who came to work on the public stage of drama had to face the brunt of patriarchal physical and political ideologies. They were held responsible for portraying the symbols of stereotypical femininity in public spaces.

The struggles discussed here through the narratives of Malayali women actors have parallels in the history of women's theatre everywhere, but many of these narratives are more complicated because of the caste system prevalent in Kerala in the early twentieth century. This is especially true for women such as P.K. Rosy, Palluruthy Lakshmi, Seethalakshmi and M.K. Kamalam who belonged to marginalized communities. In my interviews with some of these women, in their own writings and in the archives are untold stories that have not been part of the mainstream history of theatre, which routinely chose to ignore their subjectivities, labour and suffering on which the institution itself was built. Their life stories reveal that the questions of class and caste and the structural violence associated with these could not be camouflaged by the apparent opening up of the public sphere.

Disrupted Lives: Creativity in the Context of Violence and Domesticity

P.K. Rosy: The Lost Heroine

P.K. Rosy (1903–1988) was the first woman to come out into the Kerala public sphere to act in folk theatre, and later on to the cinematic screen. Her initial work was in Kakkarissi Natakam, a form of folk theatre associated with Dalit communities in Kerala, in which women characters were usually performed by female impersonators. Later, she began acting in Tamil sangeetha natakam. These experiences and her popularity then led her to acting in *Vigathakumaran*, the silent film considered to be the first Malayalam feature film, written, produced and directed by J.C. Daniel, and released in 1930. The antagonist public response to her acting in this film caused her to disappear from the public space of Kerala, and she was completely written out of public discourse until her history was excavated and retold in various forms, including in journal articles, poetry, a novelette and a film, by Dalit-Bahujan activists and scholars.

Rosy was the screen name of Rajamma who was born into a Pulaya (a Dalit community) family in Peyad, Thiruvananthapuram, which was then part of the princely state of Thiruvithamkoor. In later accounts put forth by historians, film-makers and her relatives, other names have emerged—Rosamma, Rajammal—each indicative of a period in her life.[7] In his fictionalized account of Rosy's life, *Nashta Nayika*, Vinu Abraham portrays her entry into folk theatre:

> Rosy and her parents, Pathros and Kunji, lived in Amathara until a year ago. Rosy was the first woman to perform in a Kakkarissi Natakam. It was Govindan Asan, the famous local teacher of the art form, who brought Rosy into the field. The male actors had a lot of objections about a woman performing in the drama but all of those dissipated when the audience began appreciating her talents. This was a new world for Rosy—a world to experience art. She played the beautiful Parvathi, and she loved her dance, songs and dialogue. Later, Neeli akkan told her that none of the female characters until then—Parvathi, Ganga, the Queen—were played by women but by men to impersonated women. How could that be! She was amazed. How could men disguise themselves and turn into such beauties! Neeli akkan told her that no woman

had ever performed in a Kakkarissi natakam. The Parvathi she saw in the natakam lived in Rosy's mind; she danced, sang and spoke. Many a time, when there was no one around at home, Rosy acted out the role and as the Kakkalan and Vettuvan women. There was a pond near her hut that was not visited by many. She performed her little plays on its bank.[8]

Kakkarissi Natakam is a form of musical drama particularly prominent in Kerala's southern areas. The language used is a blend of Tamil and Malayalam. The main story revolves around the god Shiva and the goddesses Parvathi and Ganga arriving on earth to end the reign of evil. However, different troupes would add their own socio-critical commentary, speeches, jokes and dialogues according to their interests. The premise is that the good people of earth, suffering the cruel acts of demons, pray to Shiva who, along with his wives, decides to intervene. Since the demons would recognize them and hide if they went in their true forms, the trio take up the sage Narada's advice and present themselves in disguise. Shiva disguises as a man belonging to the Kakkalan tribe and a snake charmer, while Parvathi and Ganga dress themselves as women from the Kakkalan and/or Vettuvan communities. Travelling around palaces, temples and forests, they find the demon-folk and eradicate all evil they come across. At the end of the drama, when the demons try to attack Parvathi, she curses and changes them all into rocks, owls, cats, lizards and other lowly things. However, feeling pity for their plight, Parvathi takes the curse back. The demons, now back in their true form, pledge that they will desist from maliciousness and will no longer cause harm, and the drama ends on this good note.[9]

As a child, Rosy had learnt Kakkarissi and insisted on attending rehearsals at the kalari, the traditional performing arts training institution. Acting was thought to be a vocation reserved for promiscuous women. 'So, when she asked permission, our grandfather did not allow it. Those were the circumstances,' her cousin Madhu remembers. 'But she went anyway, without the permission of our grandfather.'[10] Rosy had given life to female characters in some 'raja part' plays (another name for sangeetha natakam based on the fact that most of these plays were about stories of kings and queens) with the Tamil theatre company, Madurai Devi Bala Vinoda Sangeetha Sabha, owned by 'Nawab' T.S. Rajamanickam Pillai (the prefix 'Nawab' was added to his name after he played this role in the play *Bhakta Ramdas*). Rajamanickam Pillai was instrumental in changing the perception of the elite class that Tamil theatre was not respectable. He trained hundreds of pupils, some of whom went on to become famous on stage and on screen. He also facilitated Rosy's entry into Tamil sangeetha natakam after she gained popularity in folk theatre. Her theatre life and the controversies surrounding it are represented in *Nashta Nayika*:

> As her name grew as a famed Kakkarissi natakam actor, another troupe approached her—people of a drama company that followed the Tamil order. When they got to know that there was an actress from Thiruvananthapuram available to play female roles, the company invited Rosy to perform. Rosy informed them

that she will accept the invitation only if her asan, her teacher, consents to it. And so, with his permission, she started acting in dramas and earned appreciation. But later, when she got a chance to act in another Kakkarissi natakam, the drama company insisted that she should not take up the offer and act only in their dramas. This angered Rosy and she left the company to get back into Kakkarissi natakam with her asan. In turn, the people of the drama company gathered goons and started sabotaging her teacher's performances. On one such night, things got so bad that Rosy and others had stones thrown at them. After this incident, Rosy's parents decided to disallow her from acting in Kakkarissi natakam. They also decided to move away from Amathara. There was another reason for this harsh decision. Her parents had found a match for Rosy from among Kunji's distant relations. The man's family was in town for this purpose as well. Unfortunately, as the brawls with the drama company worsened, they withdrew from the proposal. Shamed by this incident, Pathros and Kunji decided to move away from Amathara and start their life anew.[11]

Rosy faced opposition in all the art forms she got involved in—folk theatre, musical drama as well as cinema. Quarrels, home invasions and moving homes as a result became a regular part of her life.

History forgot Rosy, the first heroine of Malayalam cinema, and her story was brought to light only decades later by the concerted efforts of the Dalit intellectual Kunnukuzhi S. Mani. Mani wrote his first article on Rosy in 1971. 'It was at N. N. Pillai's theatre seminar in 1968 or 1969 I think, Kambisseri Karunakaran [politician, chief editor of the *Janayugam* group of publications owned by the Communist Party of India, actor] told me about Rosy, a poor woman, a grass cutter, who had acted in the first Malayalam movie,' Mani says. 'I started investigating from then. I was a reporter then, an editor for the newspaper, *Kalapremi*.'[12] He continued his search for Rosy for many years and spoke to several of her relatives. 'It is only after the year 2000 that we came to know that she was in Tamil Nadu,' he says. 'But we didn't know where in Tamil Nadu she was. I went four or five times and looked around in Nagercoil but could not find her. We knew she had gone to Nagercoil, but we obtained the complete details (of her address) very late.'[13] The story he pulled together was published in the film magazine, *Chithrabhumi*, in April and June of 2004 and August of 2005. In 2019, he published a book on the actor, *P.K. Rosy: Malayala Cinemayude Amma* (P.K. Rosy: The Mother of Malayalam Cinema).[14] This scholarship forms pioneering work in the story of Rosy, including the history of her involvement in the film *Vigathakumaran*. To get a complete picture of Rosy, it is essential to also examine Kunnukuzhi Mani's book on J.C. Daniel who produced and directed the film.[15]

Kunnukuzhi Mani met J.C. Daniel at Agastheeswaram, Tamil Nadu, on 24 October 1971. 'Daniel had to go through much turmoil to find a woman to play the heroine in his film,' writes Mani. 'He put up advertisements in all the major dailies in India calling for actresses. Eventually, an Anglo-Indian woman named Miss Lana from Bombay agreed to act. He went over to Bombay and handed over Rs 5,000 as an advance and got her to Thiruvananthapuram. However, Daniel found her terms and conditions troublesome. Finally, she left without returning the advance.'[16]

The first women to act in Indian films in the 1920s were women of mixed British, European and Indian origins, referred to as Anglo-Indians. Since they had hybrid origins, they were deemed separate from the women of 'pure' Indian origin. In his conversations with Mani, Daniel can be seen positioning Malayali actors as different from women of Anglo-Indian origins: 'Those days were different; it was not like today when there are so many acting aspirants. It was tough to find a woman to act. Women born into good families were not ready to work in theatre or cinema then. If they did act, there was fear of loss of respect and status.'[17] When he did find someone, he did not hesitate to pay a high salary. Meanwhile, Rosy, and the two other women in the film—Kamalam and Reena—were paid nowhere near as much. 'They acted for ten days and were paid Rs 5 per day, so their total remuneration was Rs 50.'[18] As the first heroine in Malayalam cinema and as a Dalit woman, Rosy's power of bargaining for better wages compared to her Anglo-Indian counterparts must have been zero.

In 2018, Kureepuzha Sreekumar wrote a poem titled 'Natiyude Rathri' (The actress's night). It captures what happened to Rosy after the public screening of the film *Vigathakumaran*. The following lines are from the poem:

> There, in the dark of the night
> The woman who glitters on the screen
> Who is she, this harlot
> Who acts, who mingles with men

> Her place is in an unmarked grave
> But here she is, polluting sight
> Arrogance personified
>
> She tore up the silver screen, judged
> Those of higher station, the sinner
>
> The whore
> Who inflames the harm
> That will threaten Manusmriti
> This Yakshi, she must be killed
>
> The torches of the lordships land
> On the mushroom-shape of her hovel
> With it burns the half-shell of salt, rags,
> Ribbons from last Easter, rouge and kohl
>
> The night ends[19]

Vigathakumaran, as the name suggests, tells the story of a missing child. As the story progresses, we learn that the child, Chandrakumar, was abducted by the villain, Bhootharayar, and was taken to Ceylon and made to work as a slave in a plantation. The British owner of the plantation is impressed by the character and skills of the boy as he grows up there, and appoints him as the superintendent. Meanwhile, Jayachandran, a childhood friend of Chandrakumar, arrives in Ceylon. He is robbed by Bhootharayar and, as fate would have it, ends up meeting Chandrakumar and befriending him. Soon, they return home to Thiruvananthapuram. There, Chandrakumar's sister Sarojini falls in love with Jayachandran. Bhootharayar tries to abduct Sarojini but she is saved by the timely intervention of her brother and her lover. A scar on his body reveals to his parents that Chandrakumar is their long-lost son, and the story ends on a happy note.

Rosy played the character Sarojini, and J.C. Daniel, the director of the film, played Jayachandran. When the film was released, a huge furore ensued around Rosy's presence on the screen. Some were to do with the moral outrage associated with a scene—the audience deemed it immoral that the man/actor took a flower from the woman/actress's hair and smelled it. But the real outrage that would have damning consequences for Rosy centred on caste.

Rosy's character, Sarojini, was a Nair woman. The fact that Rosy, a Dalit Christian woman, portrayed a Nair woman, wearing the attire reserved for upper-caste/Nair women, challenged existing notions of caste purity and moral laws set for women. It evoked such outrage among the upper castes that Rosy and her family were in danger of losing their lives. Writing about the film and its fate, Chelangatt Gopalakrishnan describes how, on the third night after the screening, a large angry mob attacked and set fire to Rosy's house, which was nothing more than a shack. Two policemen guarding the place had to flee. The family escaped, and Rosy ran towards the highway seeking help.[20]

The incidents that followed were painstakingly researched by Kunnukuzhi S. Mani. 'It was quite late at night, and near the Karaman bridge, she saw a lorry come by,' writes Mani in his book about Rosy.

> The lorry belonged to the Paiyyar Company (a transport company based in Nagercoil, now in Tamil Nadu, then a part of the princely state of Thiruvithamkoor) and was driven by a man named Kesava Pillai. She stood in the middle of the road, raised her arms and cried for help. So, Pillai took her into the lorry, and they continued to Nagercoil. That night she was presented at the Nagercoil police station, and the incident was reported. Then he took her home.[21]

Kesava Pillai and Rosy eventually married. There is no dispute around this fact, but accounts vary on whether or not Rosy was Pillai's first or only wife. According to Mani, 'Kesava Pillai was not married when he met Rosy. He was from a Nair household, and he was kicked out because he married her.'[22] Sebastian, in her article, quotes Rosy's cousin Madhu who says that she was his second wife.

> He had a wife and family in Neyyattinkara (now in Kerala), but he abandoned them. The couple moved to Otapura Theruvu in Vadasery, Nagercoil. Rosy adopted the name Rajammal. Ammal is a suffix that denotes respect and is often attached to the names of women belonging to higher castes in Kerala and Tamil Nadu. The couple lived as Nairs.[23]

The 2013 National Award-winning Malayalam film *Celluloid*, directed by Kamal, is a biopic of J.C. Daniel. The film focuses on the story of Daniel, although Rosy features in more than half the film. According to Kamal, he did not delve deeper into her story because her life story was confusing and the facts were unavailable, an account that has been criticized. 'He has shown her not just as the actress of the first Malayalam film, but as a tragic character, treating her with extreme sympathy,' says Ajith Kumar A.S., a film-maker and writer. He argues that by portraying Rosy as a tragic heroine and the only one shown bearing the burden of caste, 'she becomes representative of caste,' while Daniel is portrayed as her uplifter, her saviour.[24]

Palluruthy Lakshmi: The Anarkali of the Stage

> I don't want to go back home; it's not that I am angry with my husband, nor do I have the excitement of being in another relationship. Sir, I can't live without singing. Maybe you will not understand that feeling. It's like how we need water or air to live! Yes, I am getting more and more passionate about it these days; I can't set it aside. When I heard about the advertisement calling for an actress in the theatre group from Kochanjeri Narayanettan, I left my house because that opportunity would finally give me a chance to sing. I will get a chance to sing in front of a theatre full of people.

More than seventy years after her death, the theatre community in Kerala paid homage to the veteran actor Palluruthy Lakshmi by presenting the play, *Lakshmi, Adhava Arangile Anarkali* (Lakshmi, or the Anarkali of the Stage). The excerpt above, where an artist is trying to convince a policeman of the importance of her art to her, is taken from the play. It was the first time that a tribute was paid to her, and it was staged at the Kozhikode Town Hall on Sunday, 4 September 2017.[25]

Palluruthy Lakshmi belonged to the Ganika caste (a marginalized community in Kerala). A talented singer, she was attracted to sangeetha natakam because it offered her the opportunity to sing. Lakshmi entered the theatre during the time of its transition and as female impersonators were making way for women actors. It was also the time of the arrival of the newly evolved Malayalam sangeetha natakam. Lead actors in musical dramas were expected to sing classical music on specified occasions in the course of the performance, and so their primary qualification to act in these was their ability to sing. The accompanists sat on the stage. Apart from the music, jesters and the incorporation of irrelevant humorous interludes solely for entertainment were standard features. The acting involved exaggerated expression of emotions.

The first time Lakshmi performed on stage was in Swami Brahmavrathan's play *Ramayanam*, with the drama committee under the ownership of Chammini Francis. The performance, staged at the Vani Vilasam Theatre in Alappuzha, was a fundraiser for the Indian National Congress, and was a great success. Lakshmi's portrayal of Seetha attracted a lot of attention. She then went on to play the lead female role opposite Ramankutty Bhagavathar in the play *Aniruddhan*, which was staged by the drama committee owned by Kadakkoor Kunjukrishna Panikker.

In 1936, Lakshmi joined the Kerala Natana Kala Samiti owned by T.T. Thomas and acted in three more plays directed by Swami Brahmavrathan. It was here that she became famous for her portrayal of the heroine in *Anarkali*, a drama based on the legendary love story between Anarkali and Salim. The scenes were mostly inspired by Tamil dramas; the story presented through songs that had a Tamil-Parsi influence, and took place in settings such as the streets, palace, garden, harem and cemetery. Later, the songs were dropped to make it a prose play. Towards the end of her life, as she contracted tuberculosis and was confined to her bed, she demanded not to be cremated according to Hindu practices and that, upon her death, she be dressed in the costume she wore on stage as Anarkali and be buried in it. Sebastian Kunjukunju Bhagavathar recalls that her husband did as she wished.[26]

Other roles that she was well known for included that of Mariyam in *Magdalena Mariyam*, also directed by Swami Brahmavrathan. 'When Lakshmi poured her heart into the character as she confessed her sins with tears in her eyes and washed the feet of Jesus Christ with fragrant oil, even the audience was full of pathos,' writes Bhagavathar. 'Once, this scene was interrupted by K.M. Varghese, a renowned painter, when he stormed on to the stage bawling, to praise Lakshmi's acting.'[27] Her last performance was in *Bhakta Shivaji* written by Muthukulam.

Lakshmi was an actor who became illustrious, almost a cult figure, in a short time because of her talents for acting as well as singing. Known for her mesmerizing voice, she was nicknamed 'Kuyilnadam Lakshmi' (Lakshmi with the voice of a cuckoo). In 1999, I had the opportunity to interview Lakshmi's sister, Karthyayani, who remembers her sister's talents and dedication:

Chechi was the oldest of us five siblings. When I was studying in standard four, she was the music teacher at the school in Mundamveli. She worked there for eight years. In those days, women were not allowed out and were subjected to strict rules. People were against her working at the school, so going to act on the stage was unthinkable to them. They thought it undignified. But chechi paid little heed to objections and criticisms. She could sing beautifully. Classical music was her favourite genre; she performed in concert alongside people like Sadir Ochira Rama Bhagavathar. She was beautiful . . . She brought us up, her siblings, as though we were her children . . . She died of tuberculosis, after being bed-ridden for six months. The doctor forbade her from singing, from performing. Perhaps it is the physical stress of having to sing so loudly on stage that made her susceptible to this illness. Chechi wasn't that healthy to begin with.

Lakshmi and her fellow actor, M.K. Kamalam, were recommended by Sebastian Kunjukunju Bhagavathar for the film *Balan*, the first feature-length talkie in Malayalam, directed by S. Nottani and released in 1938. The film explored the strained relationship between two motherless children (Balan and Sarojini) and their cruel stepmother, Meenakshi, who abuses and exploits them after the death of their father, Govindan Nair. Lakshmi did the role of Meenakshi. In an interview with me, M.K. Kamalam talked about her colleague: 'Before I reached the location, Lakshmi had already started her rehearsal for her role. She was very dedicated to her profession. Her performance as the stepmother was brilliant. She was a dignified, educated, first-generation actress who was a scholar in music. I heard she died early, maybe a few years after *Balan* was released.'

The 2017 play *Lakshmi, Adhava Arangile Anarkali* (Lakshmi, Or, the Anarkali of the Stage) intermingled elements of fictionalized storytelling with historical information. The first three scenes are based on available historical information; the scenes that follow are fictionalized renderings of the relationship between Lakshmi and Kochanjeri Narayanan interspersed with songs and romantic dialogue. The play underlines the fact that Lakshmi left home not because of an affair with Narayanan but because of her passion for singing. The playwright seems to want to ensure that the audience knows that Lakshmi was not a 'bad woman', and that she had no intention other than acting in theatre while leaving her family, despite speculations to the contrary.

This fact is reinforced in a scene in which Narayanan takes Lakshmi to his aunt's house. There, she apologizes for claiming to be in love with him. They do, however, soon develop a liking for one another. The local landlord and his assistant try to pervert this situation by claiming that Narayanan has a 'kept woman', an actress, a low-caste woman, and they also want to have sex with her. They try to force themselves into the house and sexually assault Lakshmi. When the local people challenge the presence of a woman in his house, Narayanan assures them that they are about to get married.

This scene is a commentary on the social stigma faced by women from lower castes who worked in the sexually mixed workplace of the theatre. It also points to the notion prevalent at the time that equated women actors to sex workers. The play portrays their marriage, a conscious decision, as seen in Sebastian Kunjukunju Bhagavathar's account at the beginning of this chapter. Lakshmi accidentally places a garland on Narayanan, which in effect makes her his wife with the whole audience as witnesses to their marriage. The scenes that follow depict her busy theatre life. Throughout, the play points to the fact that her status as a woman actor, as a woman from a lower caste, and as a Ganika woman married to an Ezhava man—placed higher in the caste hierarchy—added to her life's struggles.

Lakshmi, Adhava Arangile Anarkkali was a professional theatre production, and it tried to incorporate incidents in the play aiming to convince the audience of Lakshmi's virtue. The moralistic tone of the text is dominant until the second half of the play when it tries to establish that Lakshmi came to theatre because of her passion for acting and singing, and that her relationship with Narayanan was one of friendship. The dramatic marriage scene where Lakshmi accidentally places the garland on Narayanan serves to highlight this.

Lakshmi's life takes another turn for the worse when she starts coughing incessantly and is soon diagnosed with tuberculosis. The final scene of the play depicts Lakshmi in an advanced stage of the illness asking Narayanan to marry again after her death and to bury her in the costume of her favorite role, Anarkali. The play ends with an announcement that Lakshmi, the first woman to act in commercial theatre, is yet to have a proper memorial commemorating her life and her art.

Seethalakshmi: Pushed to the Wings

Born in Puthuppali near Kottayam, Seethalakshmi (1919–2009), like P.K. Rosy and Palluruthy Lakshmi before her, was from a financially struggling family and from a community (Vishwakarma) that was considered to be lower caste. She was the only daughter of Ayyappan and Parvathy, and had four brothers. Her father was a singer and an actor, and he trained his children in classical music; Seethalakshmi, along with her two brothers, Ponnukuttan and Keshavadevan, soon began performing concerts.

Malayalam music dramas that imitated the formulae of Tamil sangeetha natakam were often staged during those days, with songs composed to the tune of Tamil classical songs. After watching these performances, Seethalakshmi's father enrolled his children in the nearby art school. Beginning in her training years, and with the support of her father and family, Seethalakshmi acted in Malayalam sangeetha natakam productions such as *Kovilan Charitram*, *Gulebakkavali*, *Jnanasundari* and *Valliyammal*.[28]

It was Sebastian Kunjukunju Bhagavathar who suggested that she change her birth name, C.A. Lakshmi, to the stage name, Seethalakshmi. Also following his suggestion, she joined the Kairali drama committee in Ernakulam. There she got the opportunity to act with Palluruthy Lakshmi in *Anarkali* and *Magdalena Mariyam*. Bhagavathar praised her saying that her voice was more melodious than Palluruthy Lakshmi's, which she considered a priceless award.[29] Seethalakshmi then began working with another troupe in Alappuzha, and performed in plays such as *Yachaki* by Muthukulam Raghavan Pillai, *Prema Vaichitryam*, and *Rakthasimhan* by N.P. Chellappan Nair, and *Bhagyalakshmi* by Pottakkayath Veluppilla.[30]

In 2003, I had the opportunity to interview Seethalakshmi, where she recollected the experience of acting in those days: 'Actors and actresses received only a minimum wage in those days. I received four rupees after performing in *Satyavan Savitri* and *Nallathanka*. Adding this income to my brothers' wages, we managed to make ends meet. I have performed for thirty days a month with Bhagavathar. There was no touching in performances then, unlike today. We can show neither the plays nor the films of today to kids. And that is why most girls who step onto the stage these days go astray. Earlier, everyone would gather in the rehearsal camp. The routine was to learn and rehearse the story and songs together. The camps were usually set up in Ochira or Alappuzha. The rehearsal camp in Pottakkanayam was very expansive, and went on day and night. I have had to sing and act many songs over and over again because of the 'once more' requests from the audience. Although there were no notable awards reserved for drama performances, many artists received invaluable accolades from the audience. If the actors performed a particular scene from the play to the liking of the viewers, the wealthiest man amongst them would come to the stage and gift gold and silver medals to them.'

Several more plays followed. And in 1940, Seethalakshmi was invited to act in *Jnanambika*, the third Malayalam film and the second talkie. 'Annamala Chettiyar, the owner of Shyamala Pictures in Madras, decided to produce a Malayalam film after a thorough discussion with my brother Vincent,' writes Sebastian Kunjukunju Bhagavathar. 'The director was Mr S. Nottani from Bombay. When Vincent informed me about this venture, I went to Madras and spoke with Chettiyar. I received permission to give chances to all the drama actors and actresses of that time in the film.'[31]

Seethalakshmi performed the role of a lady doctor. She, along with Bhagavathar, sang and acted the song 'Sukhamadhuram Sukhamadhuram' (Sweet Comfort, Sweet Comfort), which was written by Puthankavu Mathan Tharakan and composed by Jayaramayyar. Seethalakshmi recalled, in my interview with her, that she was paid Rs 5 for her performance, and was given all the saris and costumes she wore in the film.

The curtain fell on the stage of Seethalakshmi's twenty-year-long acting life with marriage. She, who had stepped onto the stage at the age of five as a child artist, retired at the age of twenty-five. Seethalakshmi remembers going back home after completing *Jnanambika* with the desire to act in more films and theatre, but things did not go as she had hoped:

> My mother, who felt like I should not spend my whole life acting in plays and films, persuaded me to get married. I was twenty-five years old then. So, I agreed to get married. The groom was Kochumukkutiyil Ramankutty, a wealthy man from Ettumanoor. The wedding took place straight away. I did not expect my life of acting would come to an end with my marriage.

> Unfortunately, my husband did not approve of my job because of the belief that women who act in plays will go astray. Whenever I asked him if I could continue acting, he would reply unenthusiastically, 'you can go if you want to'. Since it was not a wholehearted response, I never felt like going either. I lived in a society that taught me that all married women should love and respect their husbands as if they are Gods. Thus concluded my acting career and my life receded to focus on my children and family.[32]

The shadow that her husband's ultimatum cast on Seethalakshmi's life was not small. Her colleague, Miss Kumari, invited Seethalakshmi to act in *Nallathanga*, and renowned drama committees came knocking on the door with opportunities. But keeping her husband's dislike of her chosen career in mind, she rejected them all, and spent the rest of her life as a housewife while reminiscing about her good old acting days.

In her interview with me, as she spoke about not being able to continue on the stage, it was quite clear how much it hurt her. 'I felt sad when my husband asked me to stop acting in plays. It seemed like my entire life was rendered useless. To tell the truth, I still wish to act and sing at this old age. But what can I do? My voice is no longer melodious.'

Seethalakshmi then began to sing the song that had made her famous, from the play *Jnanambika*:

Listen to this story! Come my friends!
Come! Come! Come, my friends!

Once up on a time I jumped
From tree to tree . . .

'I can no longer stand straight,' she said, 'yet, whenever I get time, I try to recall and sing the old drama and film songs.'

Seethalakshmi was convinced that had she actively continued her career after marriage she would have been as famous as many others in the annals of drama and film. Still, she was not ready to pin the blame on her husband for obstructing her career; she believes that if he, a wealthy and respectable man, felt disgraced about the fact that his wife performed in plays, then it was her duty to respect his decision. Instead, she preferred to console herself believing that this was her fate.

C.K. Rajam: Putting Up a Fight

'She was invincible when it came to clarity of dialogues. She also had the talent of timed acting. In addition, she had her beauty as well as her ability to sing.'[33] These words of praise by Sebastian Kunjukunju Bhagavathar are about C.K. Rajam (1920–1995), winner of the 1974 Kerala Sangeetha Nataka Akademi award, who had a long career on the stage.

Rajam, whose birth name was Karthyayaniyamma, made her stage debut at the age of nine. After receiving primary school education, she joined a drama training camp. Rajam believed that she was the second woman, after Varkala Ammukutty, from Thiruvithamkoor to act on the stage.[34] In 1935, she joined Bhagavathar's drama company,

Kairali Kala Kusumam. Rajam was the lead woman actor in C. Madhavan Pillai's *Kumari Kamalam* and in the poet Raman Pillai's *Amitha Pulitham*. She acted in the film *Jnanmbika* alongside other actors of the time, including Seethalakshmi, P.K. Kamalakshi and L. Ponnamma. She performed eight songs in the film, but like Seethalakshmi, it was to be her first and final experience of acting on the screen.

After her first husband Gopala Pillai died due to cardiac arrest, Rajam married Balakrishna Pillai. She had two daughters, one by each husband, and she named her second daughter Suprabha after the most successful drama she had starred in.[35]

Rajam experienced the many difficulties that women artists of the time pursuing a career on stage and screen had to face. The most significant and dangerous of these were sexual attacks on the way to their workplace and within it. Film historian Chelangatt Gopalakrishnan describes such an incident: 'Once when she was performing in a play in Koothattukulam, a man approached her backstage. He demanded that Rajam accompany him to spend the night with him. When she refused, he twisted her arm resulting in a wrist bone fracture. She spent the rest of her life with this fractured bone.'[36] Another time, when she was walking home after a performance, some people threw stones at her. While acting in *Jnanambika* in Madras, Rajam would arm herself with a pocketknife whenever she stepped out of her room. Wealthy men in Madras would routinely send their goons to pick up women actors and try to tempt them with money and other promises. And if they refused, they would sometimes be abducted. Gopalakrishnan writes that Rajam quit acting in films because she did not want to sell her body.[37]

For a broad segment of society, as mentioned earlier, a woman actor was similar to a sex worker, and this attitude trumped all other proof of respectability. Rajam gave up acting altogether and spent the last few years of her life in utter penury.

Shivanikutty: Happily Never After

Another important woman actor of the time was Shivanikutty, born in 1910 in Chavara, Thiruvithamkoor. (She passed away but there is no record of the year of her death.) Shivanikutty made her debut as the lead character in a 1934 musical drama production of *Anarkali*, two years before Palluruthy Lakshmi performed this role and shot to fame. She then had roles in productions of *Karuna* and *Shakunthalam*. Bhagavathar recalls in his memoirs that it was his first fall out with Ochira Velukkutty that gave Shivanikutty the opportunity to act on stage in a female role. She was also a music maestro and continued to shine on stage for over a year after.

One of the important playwrights of the time was Swami Brahmavrathan, who ensured a bright future for Malayala sangeetha natakam. The hugely popular plays he wrote, including *Vasavadatta, Adhava Veshyanirvanam, Anarkali* and *Maya*, offered roles with great acting potential to women actors. Shivanikutty had the opportunity to act in his plays on several stages across the state. Shivanikutty and Swami Brahmavrathan's onstage relationship led to a real-life relationship, and they got married. But following the marriage, the relationship changed and Shivanikutty withdrew from the stage. Bhagavathar writes in his memoir that, 'following the marriage, this fearless personality of the theatre abandoned her creative identity and became a good family woman.'[38]

M.K. Kamalam: The First Heroine of Malayalam Talkies

M.K. Kamalam (1923–2010) grew up in an age that witnessed tremendous changes in the social life of women in Kerala. The idea that the income brought home by women would help in the functioning of the nuclear family was gaining importance. The number of girls going to school in Kochi and Thiruvithamkoor was on the rise. Kamalam's progressive family background helped kick-start her public life in her adolescence.

Born to actor and playwright Kumarakom Mangattuvettil Kochu Pillai Panicker and the talented singer Karthyayani, Kamalam was the second of five children. Her uncle was one of the active participants of the Vaikom Satyagraham.[39] Despite being from a culturally accomplished family, Kamalam's father faced resistance from society when he wanted to train his daughter in music and drama, and so he started a Bala Natana Sabha of his own. Malayalam sangeetha natakam such as *Allirani Charitham*, *Parijatha Pushpaharanam* and *Nalla Thankammal* were practised there, giving equal important to literature and music. This training at a young age was fundamental to Kamalam's life in the theatre and on the screen.

In 1937, a new theatre troupe named Kairali Natana Kala Samiti was formed under the ownership of T.T. Thomas. The highlight of the troupe was the presence of Sebastian Kunjukunju Bhagavathar, who was one of the most famous theatre artists of that period. When the troupe started rehearsing Swami Brahmavrathan's *Anarkali*, Bhagavathar took the initiative in bringing Kamalam, who was studying in class seven then, to act in it. 'I was the hero and Shivanikutty the heroine, and Kamalam was the second heroine,' Bhagavathar remembers. 'She played the part of Meher, wife of Prince Salim, the hero of the play. She was naturally gifted with beauty, and her music and acting talents won many hearts. In no time at all, Kamalam was counted among the most gifted theatre artistes.'[40] They continued acting together on many stages. Kamalam was also associated with many of the stars of sangeetha natakam, including Augustin Joseph, P.J. Cherian and C.A. Parameshwaran Pillai.

It was Bhagavathar who recommended Kamalam for *Balan*, the first talkie cinema in Malayalam. She was only fifteen years old then. The shooting, at Modern Theatre Studio in Salem in Tamil Nadu, was the first time she undertook a long journey. Her father accompanied her. In 2008, only two years before her death, in the interview I conducted in Thiruvananthapuram for a monograph about the actor, she recalled her experience of acting in the film in great detail. 'There was no dubbing and singing also needs to be done at the time of acting ... I did three of my four songs in the first take; the fourth had another take because of the sound of the wind.'[41] These songs made her the first playback singer in Malayalam cinema.

'There was no one in particular to compose music for the songs in *Balan*,' Kamalam remembered. 'Mr K.K. Aroor taught me the tunes for the four songs I had to sing, and others had to learn the tunes from me. In those days, songs were not specially written; they would take popular tunes and then create lyrics to match the tune. Original compositions came much later.'[42]

Kamalam's father also had a role in *Balan*, as the servant Raman Nair. Throughout this period, it was her father who managed her work contracts and decided which projects to take on. 'Before I became mature, my father used to sign contracts on my behalf,' Kamalam told me in the interview. 'My father was an honest artist, and he believed it was wrong to break these contracts. I took after him. I lost many chances to act in films. Now I just treat them as my misfortune.'[43]

Fathers and other family members of actors like Kamalam and Seethalakshmi were actively involved in their lives and work during the peak periods in their career, perhaps also because the income they made from their profession was essential for the survival of the family. In Kamalam's case, her father's control adversely affected her film career. She was offered the chance to work in the second sound film in Malayalam, *Jnanambika*. 'Kamalam was the first choice for the role of the lead character in *Jnanambika*,' records Chelangatt Gopalakrishnan in his history of early women actors of cinema. 'But due to her father's stubbornness around payment, she lost the chance to act in that film. After that incident, Kamalam was never invited to act in a film. Thus began the demotion of her film career.'[44]

Film opportunities turned up once every two years or so, so it was not practical to wait around for them. Meanwhile, Kamalam's theatre career took off, and her role in *Balan* catapulted her into celebrity status. Crowds in numbers larger than the venues could accommodate gathered to see her perform, and several times clamoured for another encore after a song sequence. In an interview with me, Kamalam recalled a funny story when a thief, hiding among the audience to escape the police, was caught after he began crying uncontrollably watching her perform as Mary Magdalene.

One of her cherished memories was of performing *Shakunthalam* at the Kerala Kalamandalam on the invitation of Vallathol Narayana Menon, the founder of the premium art institution and one of the renaissance poet triumvirates in Malayalam. Vallathol was so impressed by her acting that he invited her to join Kalamandalam to learn classical dance. He presented her with a medal and thirty-two books as a gift. Kamalam recalled that she could not take him up on his invitation because she was obsessed with the theatre.

Until she was around twenty-eight years old, the theatre was her whole world. Her busy and satisfying career in theatre meant that she did not marry until later in life, and although there was no dearth of offers, including from many famous people of the time, her marriage was decided by her family.

The man she married was not inclined towards theatre or the arts. Her father's death compounded matters. After the birth of her first child, Kamalam found it increasingly difficult to pursue her career. Life's uncertainties came to a crisis with the untimely death of her husband. Kamalam began teaching music and built up a good student base. She was, with great difficulty, managing this alongside her career in theatre and as a performer of Kathaprasangam—popular art form that involved storytelling through songs and recitation—when she met V.K. Damodaran Vaidyar, who had come to her for music lessons.

Damodaran Vaidyar was an art enthusiast with a flair for Sanskrit and music. Their acquaintance grew, and soon they were married. Kamalam moved from Kumarakom to Thrissur with her husband and the daughter from her first marriage. But soon, her life became mired in domestic violence and her acting career a bone of contention in the relationship.

In Thrissur, she took up a job as a music teacher in a famous dance school. She gave birth to two more daughters. The heroine of the first Malayalam talkie then withdrew from the public eye to lead a life behind the domestic screen, taking care of her daughters and teaching music. Soon after, her health began deteriorating, and the family had to depend entirely on the meagre income from her husband's medical practice. Kamalam sold the property she had inherited from her parents and bought a house in Thrissur.

Meanwhile, her husband began a relationship with another woman and had a child with her. Kamalam was willing to put up with this situation until her own daughters began to suffer. In 2010, her second daughter, Meera, recalled the details of this period: Mother used to cry, hugging me in the night. I was not old enough to understand why. She was hurt by my father's extra-marital relationship and more so because this woman came and lived with us. I was happy then because I had a brother to play with. It is only now that I understand her pain. My mother suffered immensely. She endured all the hardships silently and tried to save the marriage, which was her choice, till the very end. She looked for refuge outside only when things came to a breaking point, and when we little girls began being physically assaulted.[45]

With the help of her relatives, Kamalam fled to Vaikom, in the process losing all claims to the house and property she owned in Thrissur. For a while after, she lived in her ancestral house and then in a rented house, and finally in a two-room house on a small plot of land purchased with the support of her eldest son-in-law. Her only income in those days was the pension of Rs 150 that the state sanctioned for ailing artists. Film aficionados came searching for M.K. Kamalam, the famous heroine of *Balan*, but she was struggling along, fighting penury and painful loneliness. In 1975, she was invited to act in the film *Njaval Pazhangal*, but she was, she told me in our interview in 2008, in no position to take up this offer because she was more concerned about making ends meet and worried that she had lost her acting skills.

When she fled her Thrissur home to escape her husband's violence, Kamalam had to leave behind all the cherished medals and mementos she had received throughout her acting career. This included a memento presented by the doyen of Tamil cinema, Shivaji Ganeshan. Meera, her second daughter, holds on to newspaper clippings of the function. Kamalam's older daughter, Radhamani, remembers their life in Thrissur. 'Amma had so many awards and certificates and medals and books. When he was angry, Acchan would smash the trophies and set fire to the books. We would cling to Amma, terrified. Some of the shields and mementos had silver in them, which would be melted and sold to ward off our hunger. My poor mother! She couldn't continue to pursue her acting career, and also had to lose all the reminders of her glorious past!'[46]

On to the Stage of Social Dramas

Women characters in sangeetha natakam were primarily written with female impersonators in mind, who acted these parts with exaggerated versions of feminine costumes, expressions and mannerisms that had barely any connection to the natural movement and comportment of women. Perhaps because of this situation, early women actors were forced to emulate female impersonators. But by the time a second generation of actors appeared on stage, they had the responsibility of representing women in society in the social dramas of the day, with only a little of the sangeetha natakam style combined with it. K. Sreekumar, a historian of the sangeetha natakam, writes about this change thus: 'In front of a full house, in the rousing sound of a kuzhal, as a lamp is lit, Sreemathi Thankam Vasudevan makes her gentle entry singing a song. With that, the curtain rose to the theatre of the social drama.'[47] And it brought a new wave of women actors on to the stage.

Thankam Vasudevan came into theatre after marrying her music teacher and well-known dramatist Vaikom Vasudevan Nair. Her first role was in the social drama *Yachaki*. She then joined Pottakkanathu Veluppilla's drama troupe and acted in several dramas including *Hotelkari*, *Divyageetha*, *Rajabhakthi* and *Vasanthi*. But she only acted in plays alongside her husband. Several other women followed in Thankam Vasudevan's footsteps—Kuthiyathode Lalitha, Aranmula Ponnamma, Kodungallur Ammini, Omallore Chellamma, Adoor Pankajam, the 'Ambalapuzha sisters' Rajamma and Meenakshi—and shone bright on the Malayalam stage, some for brief periods and others until the end of their lives.

At the time when most of these actors began to act in theatre, microphones were not in use on stage. They had to do the physically demanding task of pitching their voices even in scenes that required sobbing or whispering. Travel from one venue to another was by public transport; one often caught an early-morning bus after a performance to reach another location in time for the next. Finding a place to bathe and for basic bodily functions was another difficult task. As for make-up, they had to rely on the white, yellow and red powders that the drama company provided them with, which they mixed with coconut oil and applied on their faces. The costume was usually their own clothes, sari-blouse or mundu-neryathu. Rehearsals were often in a house they rented together for the duration, and they made their way to the performances in the company of their fathers, brothers or drama troupe managers. Still, it was not uncommon for women to travel alone in those days. For the majority of these actors, the income they made from their work had huge financial significance. Actors who were accomplished singers were in more demand than others. Women did not shy away from demanding their rightful wages where required. Many of them remember how the society's perception of acting women as disrespectful began to change as they became financially independent.

All of these actors became a part of theatre as social dramas became established. The presence of women characters depicted as 'attaining a new social identity' can be seen in many of the early social dramas, with the narrative progressing along the conflicts arising from this. Women actors entering this scenario were able to step slowly and constantly away from the acting styles demanded by sangeetha natakam and explore new facets of acting that were in tune with their own lives in society. The fundamental changes this brought to the language of the stage as well as to the language of drama need to be studied carefully. Most of these actors were women who had taken the dramatic arts seriously and trained from an early age. Clear changes in society's attitudes towards women actors of the 1930s begin to be visible by 1950s, instigated by changes in attitudes and perceptions towards women in general.

The women whose stories are presented in this chapter came mostly from the lower strata of society in terms of class and caste. They considered theatre as a career, the remuneration from acting helped them take care of their families, and it allowed, in some cases at least, social mobility based on their popularity. The division of private and public space was still deep in the 1930s. Still, education in the liberal arts was allowed and applauded in many branches of theatrical performance and enhanced women's social and professional credibility. These women paved the way for the next generation of actresses both in theatre and in cinema, and slowly merged the borders of the public and private spaces. Hence theatre as a medium was used in a more radical and revolutionary way in the late 1940s. The next chapter will discuss the life of women actors and singers who were active participants in the reformation theatre.

4

Making a New Malayali Woman: Women's Agenda in the Theatre

In 1905, C.V. Ramanpillah—dramatist and author of such celebrated historical novels as *Marthandavarma* and *Dharmaraja*—wrote a play titled *Kuruppillakkalari* ('Arena without a master'). The main characters in this play include a highly educated woman, Panchaamrithamba and her 'henpecked' husband. The play criticized Malayali women who embraced modern ideas from other lands and lost their identity in the process. Women's involvement in society was ridiculed through scenes of a mahila sammelanam—women's assembly—and the performance of a nonsensical music piece at this assembly, titled 'Mahilasamrajyam'—women's empire. Rumours ran wild in those days that Ramanpillah had modelled the characters in the play on certain local women. Following closely in its ideological footsteps was the play *Pennarassunadu* (A Land Ruled by Women) by E.V. Krishnapillah in 1935, which represented the anxieties of men as women attained more and more space in the public and social spheres. These and other satires were aimed to ridicule the new consciousness and identities that women were embracing.

Entirely different from these was the play *Mariyamma Natakam*, written a few years before *Kuruppillakkalari*, in 1892, by Kocheeppan Tharakan. Through the characters Mariyamma and Saramma, Tharakan set out to explore the interrelationships of the women in his community. The play was well received by its audience across several stages where it was performed. Mariyamma and Saramma were depicted as women who had an English education while also retaining the values of Indian womanhood. Saramma, especially, was portrayed as the symbol of modern womanhood. In the preface of a book-length study dedicated to the play, C.J. Mannummood wrote that it deserved special attention as a literary work that represents women's condition at the time.[1]

Malayala sangeetha natakam came of age in the first decade of the twentieth century, and its subsequent transformation into social dramas had much to do with the contributions of theatre workers. Malayali women's lives were still defined by discussions in women's magazines of the time that retained at their core the idea that men engaged in the public sphere and women belonged in the private, domestic sphere. The social, women-centred dramas of the time represented these ideologies, while also contributing to the modernization of women's lives.

A Welcoming Space: Sree Chithira Thirunal Granthasala

Many of the women who came to the stage marked their entries into this public space questioning the conventional ideas defining it. By the 1920s, the first generation of feminists had begun demanding reservations in government jobs for educated women and for representation in legislative assemblies. A central figure among these women was Anna Chandy, the first woman judge, and the first to be appointed to the high court in 1957. Towards the end of the 1930s, Chandy acted in the plays staged by Sree Chithira Thirunal Granthasala—the library established in 1914 and named after the infant prince of Thiruvithamkoor. This was a conscious intervention that made possible the overturning of many of the ideas associated with women's acting, including the 'women's agendas' put forth by reformation dramas. Through the 1930s and in the 1940s, highly educated and employed women like Chandy continued their efforts to engage their creative talents in public cultural spaces.

Dramatist and novelist T.N. Gopinathan Nair claims that it was this institution that initiated the presence of highly educated women in amateur theatre. 'Proving that acting on stage did not hurt the dignity of women was a blessing,' he writes. 'Granthasala's success in this endeavour raised the profile of theatre as a whole, enthused talented young women to enter the field with courage and excitement, and provided a path to livelihood for many. Seeds of modernisation that promised a hopeful transformation.'[2]

Madavoor Bhasi describes the circumstances that led the way to Anna Chandy's involvement with the Granthasala:

> It was a regular practice of the Sree Chithira Thirunal Granthasala to stage a play on the birthday of the king, first for the members of the royal family, and then a public staging in VJT Hall in order to raise funds for the library. In 1936, when library workers went to the royal palace with the news of that year's performance, Amma Maharani Sethu Parvathi Bayi asked them whether that year too men were acting in women's roles. Yes, they said, because parents did not permit young women to act alongside men on stage. 'Ask Anna Chandy,' said the Maharani, 'she only needs her husband's permission. And tell her that the suggestion came from me.'[3]

When they approached Anna Chandy, she had one demand—that she would not act in 'love scenes'. Her first appearance on Granthasala's stage was in *Vyazhavattathinu Shesham* by M.G. Kesavapillah, in the role of an educated and unmarried social reformer. Her acquaintance with the royal family led to her being invited to the job of munsif in 1937, following which she became a judge at the high court.

Many of the women associated with Granthasala's theatre were highly educated according to the standards of the time, and many of them, including Devaki Amma K.G. and Pattam Saraswathi Amma, went on to work in theatre for a long time.

According to T.N. Gopinathan Nair, Devaki Amma acted in a performance of *Subhadrarjunam*, composed by Thottakkattu Ikkavamma, staged by an all-women troupe founded by Thankam, the granddaughter of the famous poet Kutti Kunju Thankachi, around 1935. Having trained in stage acting under Kochachan Bhagavathar, Devaki Amma was confident enough to get in touch with Sree Chithira Thirunal Granthasala. She also acted in the plays put up by professional troupes of the time. As part of the Tamil drama troupe started by her husband, Kalanilayam Krishnan Nair, she also went to Madurai to act at a time when barely any women from the Malayalam theatre scene went to Tamil Nadu to act.[4] Later, after almost twenty years of life in theatre, she would become familiar to the Malayali as a voice artist in radio dramas. Her wealth of experiences, including being part of the first all-women drama troupe and acting in a Tamil play in Tamil Nadu, makes Devaki Amma an important figure in the history of Kerala theatre.[5]

Pattam Saraswathi Amma's acting prowess was evident in the royal family's insistence that she be included in the plays that Granthasala staged. It was assumed that it was she who 'saved' each performance. 'There were barely any performances that I was not part of,' says Saraswathi Amma. 'I was not a professional actor, and only did one play a year or so and perhaps another performance for raising funds for something or the other. By then, I had also trained to be a midwife and started working in a hospital.'[6] It was her responsibility to take care of her entire family. She went to rehearsals and performances after working twelve-hour shifts at the hospital. Saraswathi Amma's last stage performance was in the play *Ramaraja Bahadur*, in which she acted alongside Aranmula Ponnamma, Mavelikkara Ponnamma, Miss Kumari and T.P. Radhamani.

These artists were women who had acquired an education in the 1930s, held jobs, created their own drama troupes and acted alongside men on stage; these were women who were described at the time as 'brave enough to converse with ten men' and 'confident enough to make their opinions heard' and 'courageous'. History shows that their example and influence slowly eroded over the following decades until the 1980s when, with the rise of the second wave of feminism, there was another surge in the presence of women artists in the theatre. The tradition of men acting in female roles on stage continued throughout the 1940s, and despite the purposeful involvement and presence of women, their identity as actors continued to be mired in complex concerns.

Reforming Women, Reforming Communities: Yogakshema Plays

In the first half of the twentieth century, discussions about 'new womanhood', in which women themselves participated, took place primarily in five plays that are collectively called 'Yogakshema Natakam'.

Reformation movements were instigating changes within the Namboothiri (Malayala Brahmin) community which had been trapped in old customs and rituals. The Yogakshema Sabha was the central organization spearheading these changes. Formed in 1908, its main objectives were to promote English education, end the joint family system and allow younger sons to marry within the community (a right, by tradition, only the eldest son had). In 1919, the Namboothiri Youth Movement was created, and in 1927 Yogakshema Sabha began focusing on women's issues including education, ending polygamy, acceptance of widowhood and boycotting ghosha (seclusion). Radical Namboothiri youth took over the leadership of reformation and demanded changes in the deplorable condition of women within the community. It was the conviction that the Namboothiri community could effectively interact in the mainstream society only if its customs, traditions and family structure underwent changes that allowed reformers and dramatists like V.T. Bhattathiripad and his contemporaries to step beyond the decisions taken by the Yogakshema Sabha. And as far as VT was concerned, literature was the most important weapon in his arsenal.

Swept along in the current of social reformation of the time, theatre too was changing as much or more than other branches of literature. A new language and style of performance was evolving, and it was linked in service to the train of social change. It is worth looking in detail at some of the key plays that emerged from this context.

Out of the Kitchen, on to the Stage

In 1929, V.T. Bhattathiripad wrote a play with the explosive and explicit title *Adukkalayilninnu Arangathekku* (From the Kitchen to the Stage). K. Kelappan writes in its preface:

Young people opposed the ineffective learning of the Vedas. Women discarded the purdah of the palm-leaf umbrella (marakkuda) and came out into the public, joined men in attaining a modern education, married again breaking the taboo against widow remarriage. In these ways, the Namboothiri community joined the other communities in its determination to move forward. VT spearheaded these changes, and the sharpest of all weapons he used is this play.[7]

Adukkalayilninnu Arangathekku narrates the story of Madhavan and Thethi. Thethi's father, Vilayoor Acchan Namboothiri, is about to marry her off as the fifth wife of an old Namboothiri. Thethi is in love with Madhavan, a child who comes to the illam to learn the Vedas, becomes friends with her and her brother, and then goes off to Madirasi for a modern education.

As Thethi frets, resigned to her fate, her brother Kunju, realizing his sister's love for his friend, approaches the court. The will of the young people who want to move away from backward customs is set against those of the elders who are determined to uphold them. Finally, with the help of an injunction issued by the court, Thethi and Madhavan marry.

When VT wrote the play and staged it for the first time, he had no connections with the theatre. His mediums of engagement until then were poetry and novel. He had read *Pavangal*, Nalappattu Narayana Menon's translation of Victor Hugo's *Les Misérables*, and O. Chandumenon's novel *Indulekha*, and the influence of both can be seen in his play.

Indulekha was written in the second half of the nineteenth century when English education, and through it, ideas borrowed from the cultural models of the colonizer, marked an important moment in Malayalam literature.[8] In a rereading of the novel, K.N. Panicker has argued that the novel and the play had several parallels in the ideas they put forth and the story they told.[9] Both have a main character named Madhavan who goes to Madirasi, a city symbolizing cultural modernity, to study. Representing the ignorance of tradition in the novel is the character Suri Namboothirippad, while in the play there are several such characters who are portrayed as the butt of all jokes.

Like *Indulekha*, the play is set against the backdrop of the societal and ideological changes taking place in Malabar that were the result of colonial economic and social policies in the nineteenth century. Fundamental to both are perspectives on life based on ideas of individualism and free will acquired through English education, and legal systems protecting individual rights. In *Adukkalayilninnu Arangathekku*, the court itself becomes a lead character. It is through the court and the new laws that it actualizes that Madhavan and Thethi, the protagonists, are able to marry one another. Parallel to this, the play unveils a portrait of Kerala society that is controlled by caste-based customs of untouchability and pollution—a scene in the sixth act of the play where a cherumi (woman of a lower caste) meets with an othikkan (a man who teaches the Vedas) was added specifically to facilitate this. Written at a time when new ideas and imaginings about the relationship between men and women were forming within society, the play, at its core, deals with the conflicts, contradictions and confusions within traditional marriage and family structures.

A pronouncement, in scene 16 of the play, on the 'new role' of women, made by Madhavan, is worth looking at. 'Woman may continue to be powerless for the betterment of man,' he says, 'and yet, it is her stooping shoulders that carry the weight of the sacred institution of home; the tenderness of her motherly heart that nurtures the progress of society; her silk cloth that is torn to bind the wounds of the nation.'[10] Following this, Madhavan proceeds to rend his bride's veil into pieces as Thethi, dressed in modern clothes, stands with her head bowed, her face replete with shyness and anxious anticipation. Watching the action are representatives of the old order, Acchan Namboothiri, the othikkan and so on, who are gripped with an increasing agitation, while representatives of the new order—Ayyankar, Krishnan Nambiar—are overcome with joy. The onlookers applaud.

Represented alongside symbols of the 'kitchen'—powerlessness, home, domesticity, motherly heart, silk cloth—are concerns about the nation and about the progress of society. In this period of reformation, the emerging model of womanhood was a mixture of the cultural conflicts created by colonialism. The stage directions in the scene as Madhavan rends the veil reflect these conflicts through juxtaposing the elders' agitation with the onlookers' applause. There are also specific instructions on expression and costume that point to the construction, within reformation plays, of the new ideal for womanhood. For instance, the Thethi that Madhavan wants to see—wants her to become—is dressed in modern clothes, and her expression betrays shyness and anxious anticipation. What Madhavan wants to see in Thethi is what Thethi herself has internalized through Madhavan. Through Thethi, VT represents the idea of womanhood constructed within the socio-political milieu of reformation, one that embodies externally the Western model of the 'free' woman while retaining traditional Indian ideals internally.

The Hell That Is Seclusion

V.T. Bhattathiripad's play was followed, in 1931, by the play *Marakkudakkullile Mahanarakam* (The Hell under the Umbrella—the umbrella was used by Namboothiri women as a device of seclusion/purdah) by M.R. Bhattathiripad, better known as MRB.[11] The story centred on the married life of a young woman named Ittipapthi, the third wife of a man named Puthippalli. Ittipapthi takes her own life after trying and failing to live alongside her co-wives. 'There is nothing to complain about in not finding antharjanams who are able to protest and survive their circumstances in the plays written during the time of VT and MRB,' writes Vayala Vasudevan Pillai in a study about this play. 'Women's misfortunes and societal responses to them, the power of tradition, the sprouting of doubts and challenges – these are what the play is concerned about. A portrayal of Ittipapthi who advances step by step towards an inevitable tragedy, meant to instigate change.'[12]

The central character, Ittipapthi, is a woman who does not have access to self-determination and hence is defined by tragedy. It is the same understanding of women's progress that VT held in having his character Thethi marry Madhavan, a modern man. MRB fails to imagine fundamental changes in the life of a married woman, and hence Ittipapthi's problems are solved only by her inevitable suicide. The new world of progressive theatre sees her suicide, in essence her refusal to be dominated by the putrid values of tradition, as the reflection of her enlightened identity.

The question, then, is whether Namboothiri women of that time had access to ways other than self-destruction to escape their family circumstances. It was in 1929 that Devaki Narikkattiri, a woman born and brought up within the orthodox Namboothiri community of the time, was excommunicated for breaking customs of matrimony. In an interview with Anandi T.K., Narikkattiri talks about her life after having moved to Thrissur: 'The first thing I did was to dress in a sari and blouse. I began going to the temple and other places outside my home without a chaperone. I stitched up my earlobe [lengthened traditionally by wearing heavy ear ornaments] and began living as any other ordinary woman.'[13] The fact is that even the Yogakshema Sabha found it difficult to accept women like Devaki Narikkattiri. For women like the real Devaki and the fictional Thethi, the claim to modernity was confined to the idea of womanhood as defined within the reformation movement. Thethi was refused even the dissent that Devaki managed in real life. Meanwhile, Ittipapthi's fictional life was unaffected by the changes in the real lives of women in the 1930s, and she was doomed to end her life. While plays such as *Marakkudakkullile Mahanarakam* did not set out to proclaim that women's lives remained unchanged despite the modernity of ideas and institutions, the character is rendered incapable of engaging in this modernity.

The Shackles of Custom

Women within the Namboothiri community were required to cut all ties with the outside world as soon as they became rithumathi—menstruating women. Written by Premji (better-known pseudonym of actor and dramatist M.P. Bhattathiripad) in 1938, the play *Rithumathi* presented the conflicts within the Namboothiri community when such values steeped in traditionalism were pitched against the ideas of reformation.[14] The central action in the play revolves around inter-generational conflict, as well as the contradictions between two differing ideas about modernity.

Devaki, the central character, puts forth these ideas: the right to education, to cover their bodies and to choose their husbands. While the play's depiction of these ideas signalled the influence of the feminist debates of the time, it also evidenced the limits to which these ideas were accepted in terms of imagining the new, emancipated Namboothiri women. For instance, Devaki believes that there is a right way and a wrong way to do things. In one scene, to exemplify the wrong way of doing things, she invokes 'Umaben', an important signal from the playwright that points to the idea of women among reformation writers.

Umaben was born Uma Antharjanam in a Namboothiri family in Narippatta. When her husband married a second time, she left him and went back to her parents' house, an action that shocked the community at the time. In the process, she had to give her son up and face censure from the community. Her family then sent her off to Wardha in the company of Devaki Narikkattiri. A year later, Uma Antharjanam returned home as Umaben. Later, she married a Muslim man and had another son, but this relationship, too, did not last. She converted back to Hinduism at the Arya Samaj and was later sent to Lahore where she married a Brahmin. When the 1946 Partition conflicts between Hindus and Muslims broke out, she and her family moved to Delhi.

Umaben was a woman who showed the courage, despite the difficulties she had to face, to choose her own path in life. This woman, however, does not sit entirely comfortably within the idea of women's emancipation as imagined by the heroes of the reformation movement. This fact is underlined in the article 'Umade Ethathyennam' (This Food Is for Uma) written by V.T. Bhattathiripad, who spent quite some time and energy criticizing and ridiculing Uma Antharjanam and women like her. 'The fragrance of the spring of women's freedom intoxicated Uma Antharjanam,' he writes, 'and she began to wobble away from the rightful path.'[15] These lines contain the displeasure he felt with the woman who chose her own path to emancipation instead of following the progressive man along the path he deemed right. This displeasure, couched in sarcasm, was made quite clear in a speech he made in a meeting in Alathiyoor. Describing his experience of attending an assembly of Namboothiri women, he says:

> ... Aho! Look! Look at those women with newspapers in their hands, wristwatches, eyeglasses, their saris worn in the Parsi style ... Still, they call themselves Antharjanams! That woman there with the bobbed hair, it seems she is K.N. Ittipapthi, the secretary of the Antharjana Mahasabha. Ms John presided over the meeting and incited the women's hearts with her man-hating presidential address. While my orthodox heart that had begun to ignite began to smoke ...[16]

The speech from which these lines are taken was titled, interestingly, 'If Namboothiris Are to Become Human'.

Rithumathi was used to address these displeasures and to voice them through the central woman character, thus setting Umaben and women like her who chose to overstep the boundaries of social life decided by progressive men and their definitions of emancipation and modernity against women who reflect these ideals. The plays written by V.T. Bhattathiripad, M.R. Bhattathiripad, M.P. Bhattathiripad and others instigated societal and cultural changes and influenced Namboothiri communities in ways that other literary works failed to do. And yet, their treatment of women and vision for women's lives remained restricted within male-dominated ideas.

Two Yogakshema Plays That History Forgot

It was through the purposeful, feminist engagement in the 1990s, first in literature and then in other art forms, that two Yogakshema plays that history had relegated into oblivion were rediscovered. These were *Savithri, Adhava Vidhavavivaham* (Savithri, or Widow Remarriage) and *Thozhil Kendrathilekku* (To the Workplace). It is important to read these plays as products of the women's agenda taking shape in the latter half of the 1930s.

Lalithambika Antharjanam, one of the foremost writers of Malayalam literature, is the author of *Savithri, Adhava Vidhavavivaham*.[17] Written in 1935, three years before *Rithumathi*, the original title the author gave to the play was *Punarjanmam* (Rebirth). It is not accidental that the play deals with widow remarriage, a theme that those working to reform the Namboothiri community had thus far stayed away from. Antharjanam, herself a member of the community, drew her characters from the people around her. It was a time when even the word 'widowhood' engendered horror in the women of the community. For that reason, Antharjanam did not attempt to publish the play that was part of her literary oeuvre and as engaging and deep as her other works, and although it was staged in a few important venues, it did not become part of the history of Malayalam theatre.

The play was rescued from historical obscurity through the efforts of B.R. Rajalakshmi, an active participant in the feminist discussions about the theatre in the 1990s. In an essay about the play, she writes: 'It was while researching theatre performances that I read Lalithambika Antharjanam's *Athmakathakku Oru Amukham*. In a chapter titled "The Story of a Play, and of Widow Remarriage", she discusses how she ended up writing *Savithri*. For me, who was researching the extent of women's contributions to theatre, it was like stumbling upon a rare treasure.'[18]

Perhaps the last of the reformist plays, *Thozhil Kendrathilekku* was written collectively by a group of Namboothiri women in 1948.[19] This was the only play that saw these women take to the stage in any meaningful way. This play, too, was discovered anew as part of feminist research, and was brought to the attention of this writer by the historian Anandi Krishnan. (A copy of the play was provided by Prof. Gramaprakash in the beginning of the year 2000.)

The influence of early feminist thought that lasted until around 1948 in Kerala can be seen clearly in this play as it took careful aim at male dominance. Special schools and balika sadanam (home for girls), and hostel facilities for younger and older women aimed at the Namboothiri community had begun to emerge. An employment centre in Lakkidi provided training in weaving. These centres helped nurture important changes among Namboothiri women, including inculcating a sense of independence. That educated men of the community found it difficult to accept this new, changed idea of woman can be seen throughout the play.

It is through discovering the history of a previous generation that women's theatre the world over consolidated its strength and scope. Feminist research into theatre underlines the fact that there are many more discoveries to be made of women's experiences of the theatre, and where these discoveries are made, they are not accidents but results of intentional feminist quests.

Bringing Widow Remarriage to the Stage

Lalithambika Antharjanam was able to write such a soulful exposé of the experiences of Namboothiri women because she herself had experienced these issues. 'The day she got her menses, the house felt like someone had died,' she writes in her autobiography (referring to herself almost always in the third person).

> Amma cried, relatives cried, and watching them, she too began to sob. Even her acchan, always brave, massaged his chest saying it is like catching a wild bird and caging it. As far as the world outside was concerned, she was dead now. She was not to open the door of the nalukettu and look outside, not to go to the temple or sit under the chempakam tree. In the next three or four days, she understood fully the real shape of this terrible fate.[20]

Antharjanam also represented Malayala Brahmin women who had rejected the ghosha or seclusion. She was saved from having to face bhrashtu—excommunication—only because she had the support of her family. She writes about discarding the marakkuda, the palm-leaf umbrella that Namboothiri women were required to use materially and symbolically as a veil, a purdah:

> A meeting was taking place in a city not far away. Brave women, all of whom had discarded their veils, were assembling there. They wanted to go too, they had to go, and they had to find a roundabout way to put their desire into action. They set out with their umbrella and

their shroud as though they were going to the temple nearby. On the way, they threw away their umbrella, and wore the long shroud like a sari. Then they got into a bus and went to the meeting.[21]

Women deciding their own circumstances, their own spaces, and depictions of these, are what make the play special. There is the conviction that men, no matter how progressive they were, would not help bring women who desired a new way of life into the public space. Instead, the play portrays the community that is undergoing changes, and the social engagement of men and women affected by those changes. Devaki Poonthanam, the main character, the representation of the changing Namboothiri women of the 1930s, stands shoulder to shoulder with male characters such as Mangalasseri Narayanan and Sreedharan Namboothiri. It is not incidental that many of Antharjanam's short stories and plays deal with the lives of widows. 'The souls of these unfortunate beings possessed her from time to time, and she would wonder, what if I were them,' she writes in her autobiography.[22] She had witnessed first-hand what had happened to three child widows, sisters of her grandfather, and had heard the story of a young widow, ostracized for no apparent reason, who had died destitute.

Antharjanam wrote the play to be performed at the retirement function of the headmaster of Kulanada Special School, a school for Namboothiri children, at the request of a teacher and family friend, Shivaramakrishna Aiyer. Despite not having had the opportunity to watch a drama performance properly at that point, she had chosen to write about the one issue that had made a strong impact on her. In 1934, when she began working on the play, widow remarriage had not become a reality in society.

'When I finished ten scenes, Sir (Aiyer) came and took it away and the rehearsal started. It was the month of Chingam by then. Presided over by Sri V.T. Bhattathirippad, Sri MRB married Umadevi Antharjanam who was a widow,' she writes.[23]

The play, which had eleven scenes in total, began and ended with a wedding between the same bride and groom, the first time as a game that they play as children. The incidents that happen between these two weddings, that bring significant changes to their lives, form the plot of the play. In the very first scene, the play, unlike the three earlier Yogakshema plays, introduces the varied life circumstances of women. These women include those who cling fiercely to tradition; those who regard ideas of modernity with a good deal of interest; those who step tentatively into its new space; and those who embrace the changes boldly and wholeheartedly. All of these characters—the protagonist Savithri, the proponent of modernity Devaki, Kuttan's wife who, as the play progresses, discards seclusion and steps out, the grandmother who holds desperately on to tradition, Lakshmi Varassyar who defines her own life outside of the Namboothiri community, Savithri's servant Lakshmi—are fully fledged and drawn with distinct identities. They decide how the play progresses, revealing, in the process, the nature of women's spaces.

It is Lakshmi who, at the moment of the muhurtham, the auspicious time when the wedding is to happen, tells Savithri that the man about to be her husband is

Thiruthippalli Acchan Namboothiri. It is too late by then, and she realizes that she can neither run away nor kill herself. The play depicts her as a young woman who is capable of entertaining the thought of running away. (In *Rithumathi*, in the context of the play it is possible for its protagonist Devaki to leave, but she is portrayed as not being interested in emulating Umaben.) Throughout the play, there are moments where women exchange ideas and thoughts—a women's world that is missing from the other plays. The tenderly portrayed scene where Devaki comes to meet her widowed sister Savithri and the conversation between Lakshmi and Devaki in scene 4 are examples of this. An important moment of sisterhood is when a group of women who have discarded ghosha comes to meet Savithri, which strengthens her decision to remarry. The play also has several instances making fun of men's duplicity when it comes to women's issues. The effort in the play is not to create a hero character but to emphasize the intellectual and ideological world of women, especially through the depiction of Savithri as an independent woman who is capable of making her own decisions. The progressive ideas and the changes taking place in her immediate social sphere provide support and incentive to her decisions. Still, Antharjanam, while representing her own life experiences and lived world, ends the play within the bounds of tradition even as it is endowed with progressive ideology. The character of Acchan represents both these worlds. In essence, then, this is the limitation of the movement as well as its agenda of women's progress.

The play was staged successfully at the school programme. Following this, it was performed at the annual day event at a library in Kottarakkara and at the meeting of the Yogakshema Sabha in Harippad in 1935. The public meeting of the Yogakshema Sabha resisted a proposal that praised widow remarriage but still the play was well received. 'I witnessed those who had opposed widow remarriage wiping their eyes after watching the play and agreeing that widows in this situation must be allowed to remarry,' wrote one commentator at the time.[24] Records show that the play was staged at the Yogakshema Mahasabha in Thrissur the following year. All of this attests to the success of the play.

How, then, do we explain the fact that the play was forgotten by history? Was it because the writer was reluctant to have it published? If so, what was she afraid of? Was she scared of the fact of widowhood as much as the fear the word invoked? Elsewhere, she has spoken about the fear of becoming a widow as well as the reluctance to expose the souls who were undergoing punishment for no crime of theirs, lost souls hidden behind the marakkuda, the seclusion of the umbrella. It was a testimony to the fact that even after writing so soulfully and forcefully, the issue of widow remarriage consumed her. Nevertheless, this example of women's writing, the text of which was discovered and published only after her death, is one that provided much-needed impetus to the history of women's theatre.

To the Workplace

Written and published by Antharjana Samajam, a collective of Namboothiri women in 1948, the play *Thozhil Kendrathilekku* (To the Workplace) changed the persisting conventions of women's presence on stage. What makes this play remarkable is its depiction of women's mental conflicts as well as their overt questioning of family circumstances that restrict their independence. And in doing this, it represented women's public space and women-led resistance. When the character Devasena is about to be sold under the pretext of marriage, other women characters come to her rescue and take her to the thozhil kendram—a workplace for women. Parvathi and Devaki, two of the main characters, are depicted as women capable of defining their own lives as well as of supporting others to escape the shackles of and conflicts within the anti-women milieu of their lives.

Much of its engagement with women's issues are presented as discussions among women who represent a new wave, modern, educated women, and women still embedded in traditions and customs. Through these discussions, new conflicts taking place in Namboothiri women's lives are revealed. In the third scene of the play, Devaki is seen revealing her desire to engage in society to her new husband who is a lawyer. In scenes 3 and 4, she is seen trying to compromise, to find a middle path between what she is allowed and what she desires. The writing allows this character to grow organically, and by the time we get to scenes 6 and 7, we see her becoming more and more concerned about the spaces that are closing in, that are being denied to her, which leads her to question the uncivil ways in which her husband behaves towards her. The following dialogue from the play, where her friend Parvathi advises her, is an example of the play's ideological response to women's conflicts:

Parvathi: Our values are not about creating distance between husbands and wives, but about being able to live, together, as equals. We should try our best not to be estranged while being also ready, if all else fails, to take the last necessary step. In everything we do, we must be mindful of the consequences of leaving our husbands. And if we do leave them, there is no point in regretting this decision afterwards. So, be very certain. No risk is too much to escape from slavery. Just that all decisions should be taken only after careful thought and consideration.[25]

Thozhil Kendrathilekku was written in the background of the practice of giving young Namboothiri girls as wives to men of the Chettiyan and other communities, mainly to Siddapur and Sirsi in Karnataka, in exchange for money, essentially selling them. In the Namboothiri community, only the eldest son was allowed to marry within their caste. This custom naturally perpetuated polygamy and the marrying off of very young girls to elderly men, which led to a higher number of widows who were then not allowed to remarry. Within these polygamous relationships, young women suffered infighting among co-wives and violence from their husbands. The custom of parents sending their daughters off was justified as a solution to this problem. For the young women and girls, sent away to a place with no knowledge of its language and no skills or education to survive on their own, life was simply hell. The Antharjana Samajam wrote the play to expose this and other dire situations women of their caste suffered.

In raising the intersecting issues of caste and gender in relation to Namboothiri women's issues, the play goes much further than the agenda of community modernization that the earlier Yogakshema plays engaged with. Antharjana Samajams, women's organizations that were part of the Yogakshema Sabha, were already organizing work centres for young Namboothiri women as a way of being self-reliant, and also provided asylum to women who were abandoned by their husbands and families. In the play, these work centres—thozhil kendram—become the source of strength for Namboothiri women resisting the oppression within their own communities.

In 1948, the police raided the house of Sreedevi Kannambilli, one of the actors, and confiscated all copies of the play. A notice in the March 1948 issue of the periodical published by Yogakshema Sabha announced that the Dramatic Performance Act (1948) would be applicable in Malabar from 1949, and that all drama performances would then require prior permission from the Malabar District Magistrate.[26] Before it was confiscated, the play was performed on nine stages. It was not until 2008, when N.R. Gramaprakash recovered and republished it with the University of Calicut Press, that it came back into circulation. A book containing the original text, its history, and studies about the play was edited by Prof. T.A. Ushakumari and published by Samatha, a women's collective for gender justice in publication, in 2014.[27] The efforts of women from many different spheres came together to form the women-centred thoughts contained in this play. Their work with Sree Chithira Thirunal Granthasala was an important strand of the involvement of educated women of the time in theatre through the medium of drama.

Reading these five plays together allows us to see the arguments and ideology they used to introduce modernity into a conservative society stuck in tradition and convention. They argued for the education of Namboothiri women, critiqued the oppression of women steeped in Brahminical male dominance, and called for fundamental changes in the structure of the family and family life. These plays clearly carry the markers of the first wave of feminist thought arising from within Namboothiri communities. While the plays written by men reflect the idea that reformative efforts would be incomplete without bringing the antharjanams into the public sphere of modern life, upon closer examination, they reveal their gender bias in how they defined shared public spaces and modernity itself. Male ideas of reformation restricted themselves to modernizing the domestic sphere even as they denied, in a considerable way, the agency of women themselves, as can be seen from the portrayal of their women characters. The first three plays discussed in this chapter, written by men who were proponents of modernization, posed questions about family and married life and found solutions within that sphere. The last two, written by women, it could be argued, were more strategic and founded in the real experiences of the women of the time, and challenged even the 'soft' male domination of the other plays.

As suggested earlier, the contributions of women playwrights to theatre as well as to its history were forgotten over time. In rereading these plays, it is clear that they challenged not only the differences between the private and public spheres, but this dichotomy, often conceived as 'natural', itself that determined gendered roles and values. And even as they faced ridicule and enmity from their contemporaries—theatre workers and workers from the thozhil kendrams—took pains to understand the new forms of male dominance rising in the face of reformation and modernity, and to engage intensively with a modernist public. A 'new womanhood' began to emerge from the writings and collaborations of women reformers and the agency that they depicted through their women characters.

5

On the Political Stage: Women in the Leftist Revolutionary Theatre

In the first few decades of the twentieth century, as the nationalist movement continued to grow, working-class movements, including those involving labourers, tenant farmers and agricultural workers, began to emerge and grow rapidly. Alongside these movements, plays with clear political intent and messages began to be written and became a significant part of the theatre. In theatre history, their role and relevance are discussed with a great deal of importance. What was the nature of womanhood and femininity represented by these plays that incited Kerala society's political conscience and instigated a new awakening in theatre? How did this world of political drama engage with the women actors who came on stage to give life to the characters?

By 1935, agrarian workers' struggles had consolidated into a movement that fought not only against incidents of caste-based violence and exploitation but also against the existence of the caste system itself. The labour movement, although not as strong as the agrarian movement, was already well established and was an indivisible part of the nationalist movement fighting for Independence. However, beyond the goal of the country's Independence, the labour movement had as its clear objective the economic independence of the people.

Just as V.T. Bhattathiripad and others brought ideas about community reformation on to the stage through their plays, political playwrights introduced new ideas and ideologies that formed the foundations for these movements, marking a continuum in the culture of theatre that engaged with socio-political concerns. As we have seen, the figure of the woman was central to the plays of the reformation theatre as well as of the project of modernizing the Namboothiri community and the literature connected to it. Social reformers, including people like Bhattathiripad, believed that a community could attain freedom only if the women within that community were liberated, the limits of this idea of liberation notwithstanding. Meanwhile, the communist movement that followed in the footsteps of social reform movements focused their attention squarely on the economic, social and political class hierarchies that affected agricultural workers and labourers. And precisely because of it, their politics did not include the varied and specific ways in which women experienced subjugation and oppression. What, then, were the images of women portrayed in these plays? How did these images problematize those formed within ideas of social reform in the first decade of the twentieth century? And what role did these plays have in formulating ideas about the 'essence of womanhood' that still prevails in contemporary society?

These plays need to be placed against the backdrop of the formation of the Indian Progressive Writers' Association in 1935. The manifesto of the association emphasizes that the new literature of India must deal with the basic problems of hunger and poverty, social backwardness and political subjugation. The progressive writers' movement across India shared the view that in addressing these issues, it becomes the writer's duty to fight against reactionary forces and imperialism and to provide support and energy to the Independence struggle.[1]

It is as a continuation of these efforts that the Jeeval Sahitya Sangham was formed in Kerala in 1937, a union of progressive writers who believed in the idea of social commitment, who created literature from a deep interest in the bitter truths that governed the lives of ordinary people and with the specific objective of making a difference to those lives. They believed that the first and foremost social commitment of the writer, as a human being as well as an artist, is to take on the responsibility for social change. K. Damodaran's play *Pattabakki* (Rent Arrears), widely considered to be the first political play in Malayalam, the first in a long chain of propaganda plays, adheres to these principles.[2]

Theatre Work as Political Work

Making Ends Meet: *Pattabakki* (1938)

The strengthening Independence movement emboldened the general inclination to resist structures of power, also fuelling the resistance between jenmi (landowner) and kudiyaan (bonded labourer). It is this scenario that gave birth to a play like *Pattabakki*, the story of which is set against the background of the agrarian movement beginning to emerge in Kerala. Commenting on the characters in the play, C.J. Thomas, playwright and critic, says that there is something unattractive about them, and that while we, as audience, may sympathize or be repelled by them, none of us would want to meet them again. Yet, he does not overlook the political importance of the play: 'If we are to build a life based on an ideology, it is imperative that the society as a system undergoes a fundamental transformation. Sri Damodaran has succeeded in reflecting this idea clearly and believably in *Pattabakki*.'[3]

Pattabakki is considered the first political play in Malayalam because it problematizes the economic and political independence of the agrarian community based on a clearly articulated ideology. It ignored the customary understandings around the aims and objectives of stage performances. It was also the first play to embrace the Marxian idea that the emotional problems people faced were social problems and that there was an economic-political foundation to these problems.

The play revolves around Kittunni, a labourer struggling to make ends meet, and his sister, Kunjimalu. In the first scene, we see Kunjimalu returning home after wandering around the shop and the neighbouring houses looking to borrow a handful of rice for the night's meal. Meanwhile, Kittunni comes home having spent the day's wages on a piece of cloth for a blouse for his sister. He has justifications for such an action. 'Kunjimalu has just the one blouse, and that's torn to tatters. What is she to do if she has to step out? That's why I bought this.'[4]

This act, born of the conviction that Kunjimalu's dignity was more important than their poverty, drives Kittunni into a situation where he has to steal the rice to sate their hunger. Another important arc in the narrative is the eviction of the family from the land where they lived because of rent arrears. Here, too, Kunjimalu drives the narrative. Kittunni tells Raman Nair, the jenmi's overseer, that he is unable to pay the arrears. His response, a sexual innuendo about Kunjimalu, provokes Kittunni and he beats him.

> Kittunni: Rich folk think that us poor folk's women are all whores. They don't know my sister.
> Avaran: Kittunniarey, they're not satisfied with collecting their rent. They can't bear it if us folks have good, pretty women.[5]

A disgraced Raman Nair swears vengeance, and leaves promising to render the family destitute.

What is unique about this play is that the narrative cannot move forward without involving Kunjimalu: 1) Kittunni ends up stealing rice and is arrested and sent to jail; 2) Raman Nair prevails on the jenmi and has him evict Kunjimalu and the family; 3) their mother dies by the wayside, and with no other option to look after their younger brother, Kunjimalu resorts to prostitution.

Writing about *Pattabakki* in a book on the progressive writers' movement, P.K. Gopalakrishnan says, 'watching this play at farmers' assemblies energized farmers.

It inspired them to continue fighting for a new way of life. The play was testament to the fact that writers did not merely create situations within their works but instigated changes in situations existing in reality.'[6] The play helped shape a democratic foundation for leftist politics in Kerala, and the plays that followed it affirmed the belief, at least for a short period of time, among communities of workers and farmers that theatre work was indeed political work.

A Poet's Take on Social Inequalities: *Koottukrishi* (1949)

Written by Edasseri Govindan Nair, one of Kerala's prominent poets of the realist school, *Koottukrishi* (Collective Farming) is a political propaganda play that became extremely popular.[7] It was successful in fully imagining its audience and writing about a rural social problem in the language of those rural communities. Members of an old Nair family decide to set aside feudal values and family glory and work the land side by side with their tenant farmers, Abubaker and Velu. They face violence and threats from reactionary members of all communities, but they disregard all and continue with their endeavour. Simultaneously, their collaboration sprouts the seed for a mixed marriage. The play ends with the marriage taking place successfully.

For the playwright, the text is a testament of his actual participation in the struggle against communalism, reactionary customs, superstitions and economic hierarchies—in essence, in the political struggle for freedom. Edasseri writes about his political stance:

> ... I believe in God. Still, when I write about the hunger and lovelessness that have always affected me, I find myself divested of the humility inherent in theism and the respect for philosophy. Because of this, one may find scattered in the poetry of this poet who swears by Gandhiji's ideas that disrespect Gandhism or challenge theism. Some of these objective and factual writings, by someone who is a disciple of Gandhi and has not studied Marxian philosophy, have become useful in the collection of the Communist Party's propaganda literature.[8]

In writing *Koottukrishi*, Edasseri looked for solutions to the hardships he and the ordinary people around him experienced without having to support the progressive writers' movement. The play's characterization and dialogues are indicative of a poet's prowess in addressing these issues. Still, *Koottukrishi* was staged in front of many different audiences as part of the Communist Party's political propaganda.

Unlike in *Pattabakki*, women characters in *Koottukrishi* have little to do with progressing the narrative or the action, a characteristic it has in common with the plays that would follow it. Through its storyline about the love between Ayesha and Sukumaran, the play raises up a new humanity beyond the confines of caste and religion. The main male characters in the play—Sreedharan Nair (jenmi/landowner), Velu (smallholder farmer), Sukumaran Nair (jenmi's brother), Abubaker (tenant farmer), Nambiar (lawyer's clerk)—are portrayed as intelligent people trying to find solutions to end feudalism as well as to the economic problem of making farming profitable by joining up and collectively farming arable land that was until then being unprofitably cultivated as several small parcels. Although women characters appear in certain crucial scenes where discussions about economic and political issues take place, their involvement, if any, is confined to personal comments. The following scenes from the play are examples:

> Sukumaran: So, Velu, now you hold the hoe and the Mappila holds on to the land! Everything has turned topsy-turvy. Them and us, we can never get along. Never ever.
> Velu: What are you, an RSS supporter?
> (Parvathi enters. She is fifteen years old and is dressed frugally. She has two mugs and a container with tea in it.)
> Parvathi: He is RSS, etta. He's always fighting and beating up people.[9]
> Abubakker: Collective farming? Is that possible? That's what we need to think.
> Nambiar: Aavo! Who knows! New laws, isn't it? They call it pathuvaram when jenmi and kudiyan cultivate the land together. But once the harvest is over, if you want to enter the field, here, you'll have to have his permission. Ask your lawyer.
> Velu: He's another shaitan!
> (Ayesha laughs.)
> Abubakker: She is also of your opinion. The courts are full of shaitans, she says.
> Ayesha: Well, what else would you call those who tell lies and get people to beat up one another.
> Abubakker: (Looks at Ayesha.) Enough. Go inside.[10]

In the play, men represent intellect and thought, while women are relegated to representing the body and domesticity.

Two Versions of One Play: *Nammalonnu* (1949)

Nammlonnu (We Are One) was written by Cherukad (the pen name of novelist and playwright Govinda Pisharadi) to be performed in an assembly organized by *Deshabhimani* newspaper, the organ of the Communist Party, in order to raise funds.[11] It has an important place in the plays written and performed to prepare labourers and agrarian workers to respond to the feudal-capitalist establishment. The original version had seven scenes and seven characters (only one of them, the wife of the character Pangan Nair, a woman) and contained no song or dance sequence. Cherukad seems to have been proud of this fact, writing in his autobiographical work that the play was a great success despite the absence of these elements.[12]

However, the version that became famous after being performed on several stages is a different one. The revisions to the original text were undertaken by the Kerala Kalavedi in Thrissur under the leadership of Premji (M.P. Bhattathiripad, the author of *Rithumathi*, discussed in the previous chapter).[13] Comparing the original version, republished in 1988 by Chintha Publishers, to this revised version brings out several interesting factors. Two new characters have been added—the daughters of the character Avaraan, seventeen-year-old Amina, and Ayesha, who is around twelve, as well as several song-and-dance sequences. The female characters and the song-and-dance sequences add interest to the action but make no impact on the narrative which remains more or less unchanged. Amina is introduced into the play as the love interest of twenty-five-year-old Sankunni, the community-minded political activist son of Pangan Nair, and she appears in a few scenes filled with song, dance and light-hearted mischief that punctuate the scenes with serious action relating to the message of the play. Take scene 3, for example, between Sankunni and Amina. Amina is eating a mango and humming a song.

> Sankunni: Why won't crows come if there are mangoes ripe enough? This mango here by the fence, so ripe and ready, this one will also be pecked by a crow. (Laughs loudly.)
> (Amina makes a haughty face at him. Sankunni exclaims, 'Dey! Here now!' and reaches over the fence as though to slap her playfully. Amina moves away from his reach.)[14]

Overcome with shyness by Sankunni's innuendo, as Amina begins to prance away, he waylays her, and the scene ends with a duet. The scene adds nothing to the play's storytelling. It takes place at the bamboo fence between the properties of Pangan Nair and Avaraan. It is telling that the space Premji finds for women within the play is at this liminal space that forms the main narrative conflict in the play.

Amina would like to attend the meetings of the farmers' collective. Her sister Ayesha is performing a dance there. But her bappa, Avaraan, forbids her. 'Aren't you a girl, daughter? It is not appropriate for you to attend meetings and processions. Now, don't stand around here, go sit with your umma.'[15] As a girl, throughout the play, Amina experiences male control, but the playwright makes no attempt to address this. Her final appearance is in scene 10, along with Sankunni. She is gazing at a birdcage hanging on the veranda of her home and speaks to Sankunni as though she is resigned to her fate.

> Amina: Will no one open the cage? No one?
> Sankunni: What if they don't?
> Amina: If they don't, this bird will sit in this cage and sing until it dies of a broken heart. It will die, Sankunni.[16]

Avaraan walks into the scene. 'Go inside, Amina!' he roars, and the curtain falls, hiding Amina, who stands with her head bowed. She is erased by her father's voice and does not appear again in the play that continues for four further scenes until its denouement.

Two other scenes are worth looking at to further exemplify the relationship between men and women that the play embodies. One, in scene 1, is a conversation between Sankunni, who is whittling a long stick to use as a flagpole, and Amina:

> Amina: Why you have that stick? You don't keep crops or buffalos. So, what's it for?
> Sankunni: Oh, this thing? It's to tame the unruly little buffalo calf next door.[17]

And in scene 7, Amina is writing placards for the procession with Sankunni looking over her work:

> Sankunni: (Looking at the placards Amina has finished) Amina, you wrote these?
> Amina: Why? Don't you like them?
> Sankunni: (Sarcastically) Yes, yes, I like them.
> Amina: What, you think letters only come to your fingers? We women can also read and write.
> Sankunnni: Oh, taken offense already, have you?
> Muhammad: That's the one thing girls are good at, taking offense.
> Sankunni: You can barely open your mouth before they're offended![18]

In this scene, the character Amina is being shaped through the words of the political activists Sankunni and Muhammad. It is through their joviality and sarcasm that she grows into a girl, an example of all girls who are assumed to take offense for no reason, who cannot undertake tasks such as writing placards, who are as 'unruly as buffalo calves' that need disciplining. Throughout the play, Muhammad and Sankunni speak in 'proper' Malayalam as educated people are supposed to do, while Amina and Ayesha speak the local Malayalam of the Mappila Muslim community that is considered 'illiterate' and 'unrefined'. The values, customs and speech of the Muslim community that they are part of present themselves only through these female characters, while the male character from the community, Muhammed, is depicted as someone who has overcome such restrictions. This use of language is reminiscent of the rule in Sanskrit dramas that women and subaltern characters must speak in Prakrit. Through this and the actions of her father, who forbids Amina from even attending the public procession, while she is ready to lead it, the playwright casts his female characters as less than and unequal to the male.

Making Communists: *Ningalenne Communistakki* (1952)

In 1943, at the third meeting of the Progressive Writers' Association in Bombay, the idea of forming a separate association for performance arts was first discussed. The IPTA—Indian Peoples' Theatre Association—came into being on 25 May 1948. This association, under the leadership of P.C. Joshi, brought prominent classical artists and local community artists closer.

The IPTA represented a new philosophy of art. According to this philosophy, 'new art and culture should be in service of anti-imperialist and anti-feudalist movements. Modernizing political forces can look to the strength of art and culture in organizing people. The IPTA was a movement that attempted to build a bridge between culture and politics. It incentivized upper-class, aristocratic artists to learn from popular art and culture.'[19]

The communist movement in Kerala developed a programme of cultural engagement, perhaps also in connection with the formation of IPTA. From it emerged the theatrical people's movement, Kerala People's Arts Club, better known as KPAC. Written by Thoppil Bhasi, *Ningalenne Communistakki* (You Made Me a Communist) was the second drama staged by KPAC.[20] Both the play and the organization had significant influence on the political, social and cultural involvement of the people of Kerala. In the preface to the published text of this play, C. Unniraja examines the contributions it made to the history of Malayalam theatre in general and to leftist politics in particular. 'It is possible to identify this play as the first to create heroes and heroines from among ordinary labourers and poor farmers, and casting their lived experiences, their problems and their resistance, as its central theme.'[21]

Thoppil Bhasi was a writer, political activist and an influential figure in the Communist Party. He used the play to cleverly argue that in an economic system maintained by the hierarchies between the haves and the have-nots, the only option for the have-nots is to join the Communist Party. The play is set against the backdrop of the social decay of a Nair family in mid-Thiruvithamkoor. The central storyline revolves around two men symbolizing this decay—Paramupilla and Kesavan Nair—and the conflicting impact of the strengthening farmers' movement on them. The specific objective behind the creation of this play is to speed up the already well-established growth of leftist organizations and movements.

The play has four women characters—Mala, a farm worker; Sumam, the daughter of the jenmi Kesavan Nair; Karthyayaniyamma, the wife of Paramupilla; and his daughter, Meenakshi. As with the plays discussed earlier, these women have no involvement in the central action or the progression of the narrative arc. The main plot—turning Paramupilla into a communist—is fulfilled without them. What E.M.S. Namboodiripad—a prominent leader of Kerala's communist party and twice its chief minister—had to say about these women characters is pertinent here: 1) Mala, who is secretly in love with Gopalan (Paramupilla's son), and Sumam, whom Gopalan is in love with, have no role other than their love for Gopalan in the storyline. 2) If it were not for the playwright's beliefs about love that resulted in a distortion of her character, Mala would have grown into a brave worker in the farmers' movement. 3) In the story world dealing with the social decay of feudal families, depicted through the families of Paramupilla and Kesavan Nair, and the growth of the farmers' movement, depicted partially through Mala's family, the communist character Gopalan and the love stories surrounding him 'create irritations like fire ants in heaven'.[22]

EMS underlines the prevailing idea that in order to become a 'brave worker' in political movements, women had to forego soft emotions such as love. For him, love distracts from the serious business of political activism that is the main subject of the play. In reality, however, political discussions do not provide women characters with even the limited space love allows them.

Theatre historians have commented on the fact that the characterization of women and the style of writing in *Ningalenne Communistakki* are heavily influenced by Tamil sangeetha natakam. G. Sankara Pillai notes in his history of the Malayalam theatre that it is this influence that has left 'a soft and alluring strand of romantic angst, incongruent with the hard emotions of a political drama' running through it.[23] Kattumadam Narayanan accuses the play of following the convention of musical theatre that filled the narrative with as many unnecessary emotions and tastes as possible in a bid to satisfy all types of audiences. 'The only thing of note in *Ningalenne Communistakki* is some top-quality acting and some good music. It is deplorable that the tradition of the torn bundle stuffed to bursting that the Tamils began is followed in this play.'[24]

The play was written in the 1950s, when people's organizations were varied and active in the public sphere. Women had entered political space in large numbers as part of the nationalist and leftist movements. Mala and Sumam are representatives of the free, politically minded women in the changing society of Kerala. But these positive changes in women's identities are not evident in the play, and Mala and Sumam are endowed only with the old notions of traditional and romantic values.

Mala is introduced in scene 2 where she has an altercation with the jenmi, Kesavan Nair. The scene takes place in front of Mala's hut.

> Kesavan Nair: (Grinning foolishly again) Silly girl! Be there after sunset this evening.
> Mala: What for?
> Kesavan Nair: Come first, then I'll tell you. (Moves closer to Mala)
> Mala: (Angrily) Che! Get away from me, Thambra. Just because we are Pulayar . . .
> (Runs inside her hut.)[25]

Here, Mala is depicted as a Dalit woman with agency, brave enough to stand up to the advances of the Savarna jenmi man, a clear indication that she has the potential to be developed into a stronger character in the play. At the end of this scene, Gopalan and Mathew enter. All three are comrades in the same movement, but from then on, until the end of the play, Mala is relegated into their shadow. Her identity is confined to that of a woman in need of love and protection. The play puts forth a structure that endows a strength, relevance and brightness to characters that are involved in politics, while those endowed with emotions such as love are rendered less important. Love itself is a scenario where women could have had much more agency, but, faced with fiery discussions on politics, it is devalued. Examples abound throughout the play as seen in the rest of scene 2 and in scenes 6, 7, 8 and 12 that portray Mala's responses to the romance between Gopalan and Sumam. In these scenes, Mala appears desperate and broken. In scene 6, which is crucial to the narrative development of the play, and in scene 11, Mala is a silent spectator to events taking place in the yard of her own hut. In scene 6, as the altercation between Kesavan Nair and Mathew takes place, she is inside, lying face down and crying. The same woman who had shown enough courage to stand up to the jenmi's advances in scene 2 is reduced to a helpless shell of her former self because of unrequited love. Leaving her thus reduced, the playwright instead looks to Mathew to confront Kesavan Nair.

Mathew: (In a loud voice) I know why Veluchar's daughter killed herself. I know the story. And Karamban's wife. You beat her to death. That too I know. You are so heartless that you poisoned your own wife because she wouldn't put up with your horrible deeds.[26]

Mathew's speech reveals three atrocities against women that Kesavan Nair has committed, and links him to the deaths of three women, one of whom (Karamban's wife) is Mala's mother. The threat to Mala is also indicated in this scene—the notion that he has come to Mala's hut to hurt her—and it is mitigated by the presence of Mathew. Perhaps the playwright concluded that Mala was not strong enough to stand up to the cruel Kesavan Nair, rendering her, in the process, a woman active in the political movement but has lost her tongue and needs the protection of her male comrades—an example for all women within political movements. Love is rendered a tender emotion, and Mala's intelligence in being able to recognize Kesavan Nair's deviance and her ability to stand up to it are imprisoned in it. And by relegating Mala to the space of love and song, secondary to the narrative arc of the play, the playwright recreates the traditional ideas about women in society.

Children of the Revolution: *Inquilabinte Makkal* (1953)

Another important political drama of the 1950s was *Inquilabinte Makkal* (Children of Inquilab), written by P.J. Antony, veteran actor (the first Malayali to win the 'Bharath' award, the National Film Award for Best Actor) and screenwriter.[27] The play was set against the background of the strengthening influence of socialist ideology, the influence of the Soviet Union on the Indian Communist

Party, and the anti-communist propaganda unleashed by the Opposition. The play takes aim at the politics of the Congress Party and its perceived efforts to topple the left-led government.

The characters in *Inquilabinte Makkal* have turned their backs on religious beliefs they had held dear in order to work for the collective aims of communism, including women who are attracted by these new thoughts. The play also discusses how the Catholic Church spearheaded anti-communist feeling within communities. The main story follows the travails of a devout Christian couple, Devassi and Veroni, and their children, Varky, an atheist, and Thresyamma. The church opposes the education of Thresyamma. Varky is in love with Stella, a factory worker, and Thresyamma with Francis. Strewn among fiery political discussions are romantic scenes and songs. As the younger members are isolated within their family ruled by strict religious beliefs and thoughts and are eventually disowned, it is their friends who come to their rescue.

The main crisis in the play occurs when the factory owner decides to shut it down, leading the workers to go on strike. This was perhaps the first time a factory and the problems faced by factory workers became the focal point in a political drama. As this crisis unfolds, Devassi's younger son dies of an illness. The church refuses to allow funeral rites to be held because Varky is an atheist and Thresyamma reads books. This reaction from the church causes significant changes in the entire family's political outlook.

Veroni, the mother, is portrayed differently from other dramas of the time. She is not helpless or weak, and looks after the family with what she earns as a daily wage labourer. Throughout the course of the play, she makes her presence felt through her speech and actions. Thresyamma is also portrayed as important to the narrative arc and is introduced as a woman with a quiet maturity who loves reading. And while Stella is mostly placed within the softer emotional space of the private life of the male political activist, in this case Varky, she too is relevant to the progression of the narrative. It is she who explains the political implications of the factory shut down to her father who lost his job as a result.

Recalling her experience of working with the playwright, P.K. Medini, the revolutionary singer, stage artist and freedom fighter, who played the role of Stella, says, 'the play ended with Varky, along with his family and workers of the fishing industry, standing on the stage with his fist raised. As the curtain fell, the theatre echoed with the call "Inquilab Zindabad". I can still hear it.'[28] P.J. Antony was familiar with the lives of poor Christian communities in Kochi and was able to draw from it to develop his characters organically. The play was banned after a few performances, and it was not until much later that the ban was lifted. It went on to be staged in several places after that. It was not a great success in terms of artistic creativity and was more concerned with the propaganda of its political messages. And yet, the attempts to suppress it as well as its political content made it hugely popular.

Good Human Beings: *Jju Nalloru Mansanakan Nokku* (1953)

Written by E.K. Ayamu, *Jj Nalloru Mansanakan Nokku* (You Try to Become a Good Human Being) is a revolutionary play that shook Kerala's society to the core.[29] As well as laying bare the superstitions and reactionary customs within the Muslim communities of northern Kerala, the play portrayed the growing solidarity within farmers' movements.

Northern Kerala has a unique position within the history of India. It is here that the Mappila Rebellion, in resistance to colonialism and feudalism, originated. The region is home to the largest number of Kerala Muslims (Mappilas). In the 1950s, a large section of this population comprised agricultural workers or tenant farmers. Poverty and illiteracy created barriers to efforts in social reformation and progress taking place in other parts of Kerala. The conservative section of the community had a stranglehold on the lives of people.

It is against this background that E.K. Ayamu set in motion a social renaissance through theatre across Malabar's rural villages. He set up the Yuva Kalasamithi, an arts club for young people, in Ernad, and in 1951 P.J. Antony's *Inquilabinte Makkal* was performed in Kallembadam. Driven by his deep interest in the arts, Ayamu went to see the play twice. The idea of writing a play of his own developed from the debates and discussions among like-minded people interested in theatre and dedicated to the political causes of the time. Ayamu has admitted that as he was in the process of writing the play, he was overcome with doubts and dilemmas and the fear of failure.[30] Still, he persevered with the objective of recording the history of agrarian struggles in Kerala against the backdrop of a deep socio-political critique of his own community. The result was the play *JJu Nalloru Mansanakan Nokku*.

The play is set in a village riddled with conflicts between the customs and beliefs of two sects—the Sunnis, who primarily form the local population, and the Wahhabis, whose interpretation of customs and rituals is gaining more influence. It uses a Marxian viewpoint of class conflicts between the proletariat and the bourgeoisie to understand this sectarian conflict. It underlines the fact that, Sunni or Wahhabi, all members of the labouring class face the same problems, and that, even as they fight over customs and rituals, the Savarna among both sects join hands in exploiting the workers and in opposing communism. The conflicts are intensified with the actions of the feudal landlord who wants to evict the tenant farmers from his land holdings. Politically conscious, progressive citizens resist this move by forming a farmers' collective, filing cases in courts, and debating and discussing the issues. The narrative is driven by Moidu and his sons, Alikutty, who follows Wahhabism, and Muhammed who is a member of the farmers' collective.

The play has three women characters: Jameela, the wife of the new Wahhabi, Alikutty; Sabira, the daughter of the feudal lord Abdul Rahiman, who is an energetic and naughty teenager going to school; and Ayesha, an elderly woman, Hajiyar's wife, who has spent all her life behind the scenes in the darkness of the kitchen.

Ayesha, who appears for the first time in scene 3, is constantly ill-treated by her husband, Hajiyar, who insults her even in front of the Musaliyar, their guest. In this scene, Hajiyar and Musaliyar ridicule the Wahhabis, who have called for women to attend prayers at the mosque, a custom that is traditionally anathema in the community; Hajiyar comments that he might visit a Wahhabi mosque just so that he can ogle at women. From within the house, Ayesha admonishes them not to talk rubbish and says that prayers are not possible in the presence of women. Hajiyar retorts that he will talk about other women whether she likes it or not, and that, in any case, she will not be allowed to leave the house. Musaliyar, commenting on religious scriptures, says, 'women should obey what they are told.' To which Ayesha responds that she has spent all her life within the confines of her home and that all she wants now is to die in peace.

Jameela is introduced in scene 4. She and her husband Alikutty have moved to a rented house following a Sunni–Wahhabi altercation. The houseowner's daughter, Sabira, who is introduced in scene 2 on her way to school, is her friend. Sabira believes that communists are anti-religion and disrespect women. Her religious beliefs are based on what the Maulavi has conveyed to her. These are challenged when she speaks with Muhammad, her brother's friend. Muhammad speaks in 'pure' Malayalam while the other characters speak in the common parlance of the Mappilas of northern Kerala, often viewed as 'illiterate' Malayalam.

In scene 5, Maulavi, convinced that Alikutty is clueless about politics, tells him that the communists who demand more wages and refuse to leave the land from which they have been evicted are their enemies. As she goes about her domestic chores, Jameela can hear these conversations, but she has no role here or any contributions to make. Similarly, Ayesha too is outside of the political debates. In scene 6, on the one hand are Hajiyar and Alikutty who, despite their religious differences, move towards reconciliation, and on the other hand are representatives of a new generation who, realizing the possibilities of education, are in the process of collecting books and setting up a library. In the political discussions that take place, although she agrees with her son, Ayesha has no part to play.

The remaining two scenes portray discussions between a farmer, a communist and religious scholars. None of the women characters appear in these scenes.

JJu Nalloru Mansanakan Nokku faced opposition from both the conservatives within the community as well as from the government. Despite this, beginning in 1953 and over the next decade, the play was performed on over 2,000 stages across Kerala, and in Bombay and Pune. It attracted a large following, of artists, writers and thinkers. None of the members of the team were paid salaries, and yet they travelled across villages, inviting people to watch their play, which raised a voice against feudalism and for revolution.

Crafting Women's Bodies and Beings

The theatre of political propaganda and the essence of womanhood it put forth based firmly in traditional notions had a crucial role to play in shaping contemporaneous ideas about the free woman. Women characters in these plays are attributed agency, but they rarely make any crucial moves without patriarchal consent. By internalizing this model of femininity, constructed within the confines of male dominance, the Malayali female audience of the time determined a self-identity, thereby perpetuating the cultural values of masculinity indirectly.

The following excerpt is from a poem of the nineteenth-century Venmani school of poetry:

Her face, a lotus that has snatched the moon's lustre
Her smile, dazzling brilliance of moonlight
Her breasts, twin-hills in alluring dance
Who is she, rising wetly from the golden pond?

These lines are an example of the style of describing women from top to toe, prevalent in the Sanskrit, Manipravalam (a hybrid language of Tamil and Sanskrit that influenced the evolution of modern Malayalam) and Malayalam literature of the time. The poetry of the Venmani school contributed a simplicity and vigour to the Malayalam language through its use of a stylistically attractive combination of Sanskrit and Malayalam. However, the oeuvre of its poets primarily consisted of carnal descriptions of women's bodies. With the Navodhanam that started towards the end of the nineteenth century, often described in literature and the arts as the renaissance, Malayalam literature forged new paths, and yet the influence of this particular practice remained hidden between the lines well into the first half of the twentieth century.

Hair, curly and heavy, that touches the ankles; face that shames the full moon; eyebrows that render the bows of Manmadhan (god of love) anxious; eyes as expressive as those of the terrified doe running away from the tiger; lips that embarrass the thondi fruit with their redness; teeth like the buds of fragrant jasmine; throat that produces a voice as sweet as the song of the cuckoo; breasts that rise full and firm from the chest, putting golden jars to shame; shapely belly that makes one wonder whether it was from feeling inferior to it that the leaves of the banyan tree are always aflutter; thighs that have been created to disabuse chenkadali bananas of their arrogant self-worth; ankles like kaitha flowers; nails shapely and crisp as the crescent moon . . . all adding up to the exquisite beauty of the voluptuous lass who is the jewel in the crown of all womanhood, before whom even the heavenly maiden Rambha will have to say salaam. This type of hyperbolic language used to describe the female body, which transferred from Venmani poetry into renaissance literature, continued to influence characterizations of women in political dramas.

Discursive analyses of rangakriya—stage directions—have a key role in studying drama. Directive aspects of dialogue, spectacle, placement, movement, and so on, form the basic structure of the exterior design of the text. The physical, literary text realizes its interiority through stage directions, and cues for action—movement, expression, presentation—are most significant in shaping a character in the text into a three-dimensional reality on stage. These directions are indicators of the cultural values embedded in fundamentally determining the structure of the plot and the essence of characters.

Each society determines the rules of relationships between men and women differently, and these are subject to change across time and endlessly reconstructed according to philosophical, cultural, economic and political considerations. So also, studying the nature and parameters of this relationship provides us with a picture of that society at a specific time and history.

Mettlesome and Meek: Mala as Model

In scene 2 of *Ningalenne Communistakki*, the playwright's directions create the character of Mala in the following way:

> Mala is an eighteen-year-old woman who is a farm worker. She is dressed in a faded and torn mundu and blouse. She has a string of glass beads around her neck and a few glass bangles on her wrists. Hair is thick and plentiful, and her body strong and shapely from hard labour. As she sits hunched over the tapioca she is chopping, her hair falls over her shoulders. Every now and then, she pushes it away with the back of her hand and raises her head and looks around. As she works, she distractedly hums the tune of a folk song.[31]

The symbols of the female protagonist borrowed from early literature—humming/singing, plentiful hair, beauty, shapely body, the attention called to the breasts with the specific act of pushing hair away from it—appear in this political drama. This is then combined with the torn clothes and glass bangles to denote a specifically class-based description, creating a new image of woman.

Let us take a closer look at this scene. Mala resists the unwanted sexual advance from Kesavan Nair in no uncertain terms, and he retaliates with the threat of eviction of her family from his land where they are tenant farmers. Mala, a political activist, shares her thoughts with her father,

Karamban, and her comrades, Gopalan and Mathew. The action in this scene, as prescribed by stage directions, can be divided into two sections.

Section 1: When Kesavan Nair and his overseer Velu come to her hut, Mala:

1. Leaves the winnow with the tapioca she is chopping, gets up with the knife in hand, and stands aside.
2. Respectfully.
3. Annoyed.
4. More assertive.
5. Expresses her anger and disgust.
6. Does not respond.
7. Responds in a voice showing displeasure.
8. Turns away smartly.
9. With increased rage.
10. Runs into the hut.
11. (After Kesavan Nair leaves) Summoning all her anger and protest, hawks up and spits.

Section 2: When Gopalan and Mathew arrive after Kesavan Nair has left, Mala:

1. Is back chopping the tapioca.
2. Gets up. Happiness, as well as a pale shadow, on her face.
3. Bends to the winnow and begins to chop the tapioca again.
4. From that position, raises her eyes and gives Gopalan a pretty smile.

5. Sits back down and continues her task.
6. Smiles.
7. Continues to smile as she goes inside the hut.
8. Comes back with some cooked tapioca.
9. Drops it into Mathew's hands.
10. Stands aside, smiling.

In addressing her class enemy, Mala is mettlesome, capable of expressing anger, disgust and displeasure, while before her comrades in the political movement, she is a meek, smiling woman preparing and cooking tapioca. Both sets of actions noted above describe female presence as realized through male gaze, a presence that, regardless of contexts of class enmities or solidarities, is limited within the bounds of a male point of view and satisfy men's subconscious sexual desires.

These models of womanhood, shaped within leftist theatre, were carried into the realm of political activism and ideas of womanhood that existed within that space. She was expected to embody anger, protest and passion for the cause in the public spaces of political involvement, while continuing to fulfil traditional roles within the domestic space. In essence, the model of 'new' womanhood created by leftist politics through its cultural engagements was only a slightly revised version of the old, traditional model.

The Good Mother

Mothers in these plays are painted more or less in the same hues. In *Pattabakki*, Cherottiyamma is a thin, tired woman of forty; Kaliyamma in *Nammalonnu* is a fifty-year-old woman dressed in a dirty mundu and torn rowka; Kalyaniyamma in *Ningalenne Communistakki* is a woman grown old before her time, dressed in a soot-smeared mundu and an old-fashioned blouse. Only the mother in *Koottukrishi*, Lakshmiyamma, is drawn differently—she is the matriarch of a well-to-do tharavad, and is dressed in a clean mundu and onnara (the undercloth worn mainly by women of upper castes). With the exception of Lakshmiyamma, all the mothers are women beaten down by the circumstances of their lives.

All these mothers support their sons who are progressive, even as they are themselves characterized as fulfilling maternal roles set in tradition. Kaliyamma and Kalyaniyamma do come to the stage towards the end to raise their voices against the atrocity of the landlords and the eviction. And it is only in these moments that they are allowed outside their domestic spheres. Both these characters, through their actions in these final scenes, show that they had, all along, the potential to be characters driving the narrative. And yet they are destined to play the roles of mothers exhausted from taking sides in the conflicts between conservative fathers and progressive sons, walking the thin line between protecting their sons and not angering their husbands. They are keepers of their sons' political activities, social commitments and progressive thoughts. In the process, the playwrights confine them to the expected realms of activity, thereby recreating and reinforcing the model of good motherhood.

A closer analysis of the stage directions that control the actions of Kalyaniyamma in *Nammalonnu* exemplifies these conclusions. In the first scene, her external actions include picking up the fronds and sheaths that have fallen off the coconut tree, bringing a jug of water for the men, placing plates of kanji and chammanthi before them, cleaning up after they have eaten and so on. As she goes about these tasks, she is also engaged in acting as a mediator between them as their discussions heat up. Her expressions and emotions while fulfilling this role are also specified by the playwright, and these include humility, sadness, complaint, blowing nose and crying, respect, placation and so on. And through these external and internal characteristics, she embodies elements of the 'good mother' model that has existed in literature throughout time.

In the Shadow of Her Brother

Sisters exist as key characters in most of these plays—Kunjimalu in *Pattabakki*, Parvathi in *Koottukrishi*, Ayesha in *Nammalonnu*, Meenakshi in *Ningalenne Communistakki*—and yet, only Kunjimalu has a serious role in driving the plot forward, growing and changing as the narrative progresses. Meanwhile, Parvathi, Ayesha and Meenakshi are directed by the playwrights to sing, dance and be mischievous, while inserting light-hearted commentary in scenes between the male protagonist and his female lover. In this way, their primary role is to provide light relief in between serious matters. They have no connection with the plot and their absence from the plays would make no difference to the successful completion of their narratives. They are ardent worshippers of their brothers and a helpful hand for their mothers. They would like to participate in social activities from under the protective shadows of their brothers, but they undergo absolutely no transformation as the play progresses, and remain, only, naughty younger sisters.

A divergence from these model sisters is Kunjimalu in *Pattabakki*. In the absence of her brother, in order to look after her family, she resorts to prostitution. Later on, after her brother returns from prison, she joins him in the movement for social change. Asking why Kunjimalu was portrayed as having a crucial role in this play takes us to the influence social reformation plays had on political propaganda plays. *Pattabakki* was written eight years after the first social reformation play, *Adukkalayilninnu Arangathekku*, was written. V.T. Bhattathiripad wrote this play, as we have seen, as a part of the efforts to bring Namboothiri women out of the kitchen and to the (world) stage. The culmination of these efforts, in VT's imagination, was for the woman to wed a suitable man who stood firmly in the public space. Kunjimalu, meanwhile, is endowed a place outside of the kitchen right at the beginning of the play, and she becomes part of the plot of the play. This element of reformation plays that influence *Pattabakki* has been lost to the other plays that followed.

Woman without a Male Protector

As already discussed, Kunjimalu becomes a prostitute in the course of the play, having no other option to save her family from starving to death. Her protector, her brother, is in prison at this moment. Her mother dies destitute, and she is left with the sole responsibility of providing for her younger brother, Balan. It is this lack of male protection that forces her into prostitution. The playwright's conviction that it is a profession that no woman should have to go into is voiced through the character, as exemplified in this soliloquy:

> Ha! How horrible it is, a prostitute's performance of a life! How unsightly the artificial colours that she has to smear on her face. And how many men she has to trap like moths in the fiery flame of her beauty. (In a disgusted voice) What a despicable life . . .[32]

The idea that women are solely responsible for the existence of prostitution is reinforced here; men are only innocent moths caught in the fire of women's vile beauty. The playwright goes further and makes her curse herself, calling herself a shameless harlot for having sold her honour, a sinner, and a soul that even hell would find disgusting. Parallelly, this truth is also voiced: 'I can't stop this transaction. If I stop selling my body even for a single day, my Balan would go hungry.' [33] The anxiety of the playwright in wanting to reinforce that prostitution, even though Kunjimalu has to resort to it as part of the play's narrative, is not a model to be emulated is clear in these scenes. It is this anxiety that drives him when he makes Kittunni—who was already portrayed at the beginning of the play as a man more concerned with his sister's reputation than with food in their bellies—call his sister a 'whore who has sold her dignity' in the last scene.

Kittunni reconciles with his sister and agrees with her opinion that it is the atrocities perpetrated by the jenmis that drive people like her to prostitution. The play concludes, through this brother and sister, that this situation can only be changed if there are structural changes, and that brothers and sisters who go through these experiences are, beyond gendered and caste-based discrimination, socially equal. But the curtain does not fall there. It falls when Kittunni tells Kunjimalu that he will tell her how to seek revenge and restructure the systems of oppression that keep them down. 'Come with me, I'll tell you,' he says, and that is when the final curtain falls. The 'I' of male action and leadership leaves the stage intact with Kunjimalu as its willing follower.

In the political propaganda plays discussed here, Kunjimalu is the only character who is a prostitute. She is also the only woman character who stands on her own feet, fighting against poverty and looking after her family. It lays bare the playwright's ideas about women's bodies and identities, and perhaps this characterization is influenced by the traditional equation: independent woman = loose woman. It also exposes the anxiety that a woman who enters the stage (world) alone has no option but to sell her body.

Women in Early Leftist Cultural Scene

We have thus far looked at women characters and ideas about women's identities, roles and position in society that emerged from the way they were conceived in political propaganda theatre. Women's agency in these plays is restricted to making decisions within the parameters allowed by male domination; their survival is predicated on established patriarchal structures. What of the real women of the time, especially those who acted in these roles? How do they reconcile or deviate from these characters in their own engagement within society and with politics?

In the 1940s, when the undivided Communist Party formed a cultural centre in Alappuzha, women workers became part of its activities. Their participation was their political duty as prescribed by the party, and was primarily in the form of singing revolutionary songs in public meetings. Prominent among these women were Meenakshi, Anasuya and P.K. Medini. Meenakshi, armed with the training in classical music received from her father, led this effort and taught revolutionary songs. Dressed in men's attire of a mundu and shirt, she engaged in clandestine political activities during the night and singing songs that strengthened the party's ideology during the day. All three women were brilliant singers who had been denied the opportunity for education because of economic deprivation, and at various points had been arrested for their songs.

The entry of women into political theatre was a continuation of such activities. The paths that led them there varied. Two early actors, Sulochana and Sudharma, were involved in cultural activities before coming into KPAC, the Communist Party's organized theatrical movement. It is their love for performing and talent in singing that brought them to theatre. Sudharma, who had acquired the qualification 'Ganabhushanam' from the Thiruvananthapuram Music Academy,[34] has said that it was her personal leaning towards communist ideology that made her accept the invitation to join KPAC, although she found it hard to reconcile with the social identity of an 'actress'.[35] She had had a previous experience with theatre where a fellow actor had become pregnant at the rehearsal camp. The incident left a deep impression that followed her to the KPAC camp and led her to write a letter to K. Balakrishnan—politician, publisher and one of the founding leaders of the Revolutionary Socialist Party (RSP)—whom she worshipped. The eight-page letter laid out the 'actress/communist' dichotomy and the conflicts it created within her. 'Be very careful of your steps,' he wrote back. 'It is easy to lose your footing. And if you fall, those who are watching will only laugh while you might sustain wounds that remain forever.'[36] She went through her acting life convinced that a woman actor's path was always treacherous and resolving to be careful.

Sulochana—who would become famous as actor and playback singer 'KPAC Sulochana'—came into theatre because of her desire to sing and act, and the poverty that she experienced. 'My father Kunjoonju was a pukka Congress supporter and a government employee. Imagine allowing his daughter to go off with the Community Party! Of course he was livid,' she recalled. 'But he was quite unwell and could no longer look after the family, and my brother was only seven years older than me. In the end, with no other income, and with the persuasion of my siblings, he agreed.'[37]

An actor that followed these women is Vijayakumari, who is still active in theatre and television. She came into acting persuaded by Sudharma, and recalls the incident:

> I was aged eleven then, studying third form at the Cantonment School. Sudharma was my cousin, the daughter of my appachi, and was working as a music teacher after completing her Ganabhushanam. One

day she came home and said, 'There is this play in which a lot of famous actors are involved. They need someone to play a child. You must come.' My amma had no objection—she was an RSP supporter even in those days. And Acchan was a communist, but he was not happy to send me to act on stage. Sudharmakka and everyone else begged him, said these are not theatre people but party activists, the play is written by none other than Thoppil Bhasi and so on and so forth until he was convinced. Then Kambisseri (Kambisseri Karunakaran, chief editor of *Janayugam* group of publications owned by the Communist Party) and another person came to my school, and decided I was suitable to play the part.[38]

In Nilambur, as the Yuvajana Kalasamithi prepared to perform *Jju Nalloru Mansanakan Nokku*, they were convinced that women characters were incomplete when performed by men, which led them to look for women to act in these roles. This was how the famous actor Nilambur Ayisha came on to the stage. Writing in her autobiography *Jeevithathinte Arangu*, she recalls: 'My brother was getting more and more interested in theatre, and he was associated with the Communist Party. And through him, our family also became communist.'[39] And so when he and the playwright E.K. Ayamu who was his friend asked her, she agreed.

It is clear that all these women who got involved in leftist cultural activities were persons with their own will and opinions. The paths that brought them to this work were indeed different, and as they went forward, they enthusiastically embraced the political ideology of communism.

Sulochana, who performed the role of Sumam in *Ningalenne Communistakki*, remembers those times and the responses they had: 'Jenmis and their gundas threatened us and attacked us. In some places, they damaged our vehicles. In Kilimanoor, a group of gundas attacked our vehicle and came to the stage ready to harm the actors.' As a woman actor, she had to endure further indignities in society. 'My relatives considered me, a woman who went to act in plays, and that too with communists, to be an embarrassment,' she continues. 'They refused to let me into their homes. Entertained the kind of extreme enmity that made them want to spit when they saw me. I had to have security to protect me from anti-communist mobs.'[40]

Sudharma balanced her acting alongside her job as a music teacher, spending her days at the school and her evenings at the theatre. In her interview with Muralidharan Nair, she says: 'After a few days, people got upset. I was teaching music then. The government issued several notices warning me not to continue my acting. Still, I continued, overtly and covertly, forgetting my physical as well as mental exhaustion in the headiness of those days.'[41]

Medini played Stella in *Inquilabinte Makkal*. Stella is in love with Varky, a stubborn social and political activist. The character was played by P.J. Antony, the author of the play. In one scene, Medini was required to sing a romantic song and act intimately with Antony which she found difficult in the beginning. Antony would urge her, 'bring in the romance; stop being Comrade Medini,' she recalled in an interview later in her life. 'The next day, when I came back to my hometown with sleepy eyes and leftover make-up, I heard hurtful comments,' she remembered. '"Oh, here comes the drama star, where were you yesterday?" Many believed that actresses were distrustful harlots. What hurt more was the fact that most of them were people we knew. But I did not dwell on it. I knew that what I was doing was for the good, for the movement, for the oppressed.'[42]

Society's response to Nilambur Ayisha as a stage actor was even more extreme. Ayisha, from Ernad taluk in Malabar, entered the theatre during the second half of the twentieth century. This was a time when Muslim women had less social engagement compared to that of Hindu and Christian women. This, coupled with the fact of acting on stage, made it inherently dangerous, even to her life. In 2005, I had the opportunity to write the preface to Ayisha's memoir, *Jeevithathinte Arangu*. In our long conversation in preparation for this, she shared memories of her life on stage, especially the sense of imminent danger always surrounding it. 'A section of the community refused to let me into their homes, while others refused me food,' she told me. 'I understood these responses emerged from the fear of going against customs. I was not allowed to attend special occasions or celebrations, and even if I did, I had to stand aside like a criminal constantly under surveillance. Even some shops refused to sell goods to me. In all, a kind of community ostracization.' She was well aware that theatre was also in service of the Communist Party's growth. She attended study classes organized by the party, spoke at public meetings against feudalism and religious fundamentalism, and by acting in the same drama on over 1500 stages, she became a 'leftist stage actor' in its full sense.

All through this period, she continued acting without being paid for her work even as she endured poverty. 'For us, all of it was part of working for the party,' she told me. 'We walked in the blazing sun, singing songs. Went all the way to Malappuram by foot, carrying the tabla and harmonium on our heads and shouting slogans. The measly sums we earned performing the play went to the party; the actors were not paid. And we were happy with that.'

Despite dedicating their lives to political and cultural work, taking on the two dangerous identities of political activist and actor, and work that adversely affected their health, social position and economic situation, they had to endure serious disappointments in these spaces in which they had placed their faith.

After the split in the Communist Party, Medini stood by the CPI (Communist Party of India). She lost her husband, and when it became difficult to provide for her small children, she took a job with Kerala Spinners, a spinning and weaving factory. When I interviewed her, she told me that it was C. Achutha Menon, chief minister of Kerala at the time, who helped her get this job. The vibrant political-cultural space of the 1940s, when she first got involved in politics, gradually began to disintegrate, and she continued trying to balance her political work with her familial responsibilities. However, she does not, in any of her interviews, talk about gender as an element that affected her life.

Sudharma, on the other hand, spoke out right from the beginning about the differences she had with KPAC. 'In those days, there was this custom, that after every five performances, the sixth would be done for free. We thought the money from the sixth play, our wages, went to the party. We didn't realize until later that this money actually went into some people's pockets. When I returned after a break, I felt I had to ask for some accounting. I am a communist who grew up within the party's strict discipline, learnt to be self-critical. No matter who was involved in the wrongdoing, I was always ready to question that.'[43] She made her opinions known, and when she felt that she was not being taken seriously, she had no qualms about resigning and leaving KPAC. Through her actions, she dismantled the idea that an actor's role ends with playing her part in the play and accepting whatever she is paid.

It was the negative experiences that made Sulochana, too, leave KPAC. 'The Communist Party was a huge part of my life,' she said when I interviewed her for the documentary, *Penmalayalam*. 'And I can't explain the extent of atrocities that we, including myself, put up with for its sake. All we did, the singing and the acting, it was all for the party.'

The split in the party had a significant impact on Nilambur Ayisha's life too. According to her, the party did not do enough to sustain the Yuvajana Kalasamithi in Nilambur. 'There was a time when Kalasamithi work, drama, political work were all so active and energetic. But with E.K. Ayamu's death, everything stopped. Kalasamithi became inactive and no one came to take its work forward, not even the party. I became isolated. I was already isolated in the community. The way forward was paved with untold miseries.'[44] The mental anguish led her to hate even the word 'drama', she writes.

What she expresses here is not merely the sadness of an actor who loses her troupe. Arguably, she would not have had much difficulty in finding a place in another drama troupe. What it underlines is the experience that too many of these women actors went through, the rejection by the political-cultural space that they had helped build at great cost to their own personal safety. It is this situation that precipitated Nilambur Ayisha's flight to the Gulf, leaving her acting, her politics and Kerala itself, behind; that made Sudharma and Sulochana leave KPAC. For over twenty years, Ayisha worked as a domestic help in the Gulf. After returning to Kerala, she wrote her memoir, *Jeevithathinte Arangu*, which was published in 2005. 'After encouraging and building up for a long time, you are abandoned. The rest is up to you, they seem to say. All political parties behaved in this way towards women,' she writes.[45] Until their death, this sentiment was shared by Sudharma and Sulochana, a fact they reflected in the words filled with disappointment they left behind. Ayisha does survive these experiences, coming back to acting and political life after her exile in the Gulf.

Beyond the space of the theatre, some of these actors continued their journeys as revolutionary artists into political participation. Their lives were inextricably tangled with theatre, music and politics, having spent two or three decades in its service. And they were, in the end, able to forge a deep social identity different from those represented by the characters they played.

At the age of fifty-five, P.K. Medini stood for the election as a candidate for Manacheri village panchayat president. For this woman from a marginalized community, involvement in leftist political and cultural spaces provided the opportunity to disrupt the domestic-conjugal myth and to strengthen her agency. It precipitated new social and ideological convictions that led to her emergence as a new cultural worker. Her campaign meetings turned into important political occasions, and her open interaction with the audience, without special make-up or costume, changed public perceptions about the social role and position of women who were singers and actors.

The path that Sulochana forged was different from Medini. When the Thiruvithamkoor-Kochi state legislative assembly elections were announced, and Thoppil Bhasi—the author of *Ningalenne Communistakki*—stood as a candidate in Bharanikaav constituency, KPAC supported him by organizing song performances at his campaigns across the constituency. Those days made her realize how much the public appreciated her and her music, and the political possibilities of those songs. Her work was instrumental in attracting and organizing farmers and workers around the communist ideology. Thoppil Bhasi had a landslide victory in the elections. Energized with this victory, other members of KPAC stood for the 1957 elections. This was a period of tiring yet inspirational activism. By 1963, the Congress government was in power, and they brought in economic measures that adversely affected political propaganda theatre. A new tax meant that professional theatre companies had to give up 45 per cent of their income from ticket sales. Even an increase in bus fares saw artists travelling with their instruments having to shell out extra ticket costs. Sulochana was at the frontline of KPAC members who protested against the injustice of the government and the ruling class and wrote an open letter to the home minister.[46]

In 1965, following some internal disagreements, Sulochana left KPAC. She rejoined the organization in 1975 but left soon after saying that she found the atmosphere strange. Her styles of singing and acting marked a new space and a departure in public assumptions about professional women actors. She dedicated the rest of her life to her creativity and talent, and used them in the service of political activism.

Even as they attained fame as politically conscious artists and had a large following of art lovers, these women found themselves more or less isolated in their private lives. Men who shared their political ideology, even their male colleagues, could not imagine making a female stage actor their life partner. While their public lives were often celebrated, they were unwanted in the context of family and domestic life.

Medini was well aware that she would not be sought after as a marriage partner given her public life in political activism and on stage. She would later marry a relative, a Congress supporter. After his death, she faced extreme hardship for a period of time. She remembers walking for seven-and-a-half hours straight as part of her job at Kerala Spinners, doing the rounds of thirty spinneries. Carrying bags of cotton and working in a dusty environment left her with declining health and respiratory issues.[47]

Talking to me for the documentary, *Penmalayalam*, Sulochana recalls 30 August 1981 as an unforgettable day. 'It was the day of my wedding. It was late in life, but there were many reasons for taking this decision, including the death of my father and the heart attack that my brother suffered. I was forty-five years old by then. Kaleshan, my husband, was a distant relative of mine, and was an artist and worked as a conductor in a KSRTC bus. This, our late wedding, was a small function with a few invited guests. I was with Kadambari Theatres in Kollam then, acting in the play *Kadinjan*.'

After her marriage, Sulochana began to give music performances of the songs from her old plays. Later, she would establish the drama troupe Samskara. Slowly, however, her activist identity eroded and was forgotten by the end of her life. In 1997, Kerala Sangeetha Nataka Akademy honoured her contributions to theatre with a fellowship.

What struck me the most in my conversations with Nilambur Ayisha was the freedom and happiness she expressed in being able to live her life alone. Although she was happy that many of her colleagues eventually got married, she was disturbed by the fact that marriage seemed to drive women actors and activists into the home and away from the stage, that no one seemed to acknowledge that marriage made a woman actor's career more complex than it already was. She believes that her independent and ascetic life has allowed her to cultivate friendships without interference from society or family that other women have had to deal with.

The stories of these women have in common their desire for being involved in political and cultural institutions and activism, the joy they derived from it and from whatever public acceptance they experienced. They are considered to have mirrored the public's issues and interests in political and cultural spheres at a specific moment in history. In Kerala, they are, till today, thought of fondly and with nostalgia. While their contributions have not disappeared from collective public memory, they were marginalized in their own lifetime. Their memoirs and reminiscences deconstruct the ideas that underline the writing of theatre history, and they need to be read alongside these histories that see theatre primarily as a public space for male transactions.

6

A Balancing Act: The Theatre as Workplace

From the year 2000, I have spoken with over a 100 women actors in professional theatre, gathering their experiences through one-to-one interviews and through informal conversations as colleagues working in the same space. Several of them also contributed by answering questionnaires that I sent them. The following are some excerpts from these conversations:

> 'Instead of nurturing the creative talents of a young person who enters this space and helping her become the best actor she could be, they groom her for other things. Expensive jewellery, clothes, amenities, she's given it all if she goes along. The owner of the troupe, the writer, the director—all of them are complicit. Why? Because they think they can also have a go every now and then. If any self-respecting woman raises her voice against this, she's then portrayed with the rest of the company as this "difficult thing". Shunned by

everyone else, misunderstood, subjected to indignities . . . her chest is pried open and a lifetime's hurt placed there before she is dismissed. Who got us here, to this situation where a woman's soul is crucified so?'

'I was part of a group in 1998–1999. They came in December and pressed me to join even though I was not keen, more because it was way too far from home. I didn't want to leave my kids alone. So they said they'd get them admission in a boarding school near the company. I agreed finally and went for rehearsal. I had to act exactly as the director showed me, they said. No one can copy another exactly, can they? My character dies in the middle of singing a song. I was asked to act out the panic of dying while continuing to sing. How can you continue singing when you are dying! Besides, the recorded version of the song, to which I'm supposed to be acting, has no indication that the character is dying. It is just a smooth rendition. Then the director and the owner of the troupe said the audience at the back of the theatre couldn't see my lip movements. I was so upset with all this. Finally, the director says he can't work with me, and so I was sent away with the label that I was a terrible actor. The year after that, to another troupe, moving the children to yet another school . . .'

'Most company owners dance to the director's tune. If the director dislikes you, you've had it. You'll be stood on the stage and tortured. At least, that's been my experience. I am not saying all directors are like that, I'm sure there are directors who are not like that.'

'Last year, an amateur company in my place invited me to be part of a play that they were putting up for the Sangeetha Nataka Akademi's competition. All of them, people I know and are quite close to me. We came first in the southern region, and of course got selected for the state-level competition. But the Akademi delayed the competition, and by the time it came around, I was acting in another play. I told my new troupe about this, and everyone agreed that I should go. I trained another actor, a friend of mine, to take on my role. But when it was time to go to the competition, the owner changed his mind, said he can't have a substitute and that I should stay and do my role. I was in a dilemma. Our slot in the competition was at 2 p.m. My colleagues agreed that I would be able to do the play and get back in time for our show. But it so happened that even though I had hired a car at my own expense, I was late in getting back and the play had to be cancelled that day. The day after that, when we were all in the vehicle going back after our show, everyone began shouting at me. One of them—much junior to me—began to speak in very objectionable terms to me. The whole thing almost got to fisticuffs. Then this began to be shown on stage too. He had the role of a villainous character and there is a scene where he grabs me. He would grab my hand and twist it so hard. After every show, my hand would be red and swollen and hurting. I don't know how I finished that season.'

'There are male actors who would sit in the company vehicle drunk and spew obscenities. No consideration for the women with them. We women have to put up with such behaviour too.'

These first-hand experiences shed light on the specific circumstances under which women actors negotiate their workplace and expose an intimate view of theatre that is often hidden from scrutiny.[1]

There is freedom inherent in the role of an actor. However, women actors make the society uncomfortable precisely because of this freedom, because they are engaging in work that is unlike other jobs assigned to women by norms and tradition. The social interactions of a woman actor in her workplace, her labour and her independence are all different from that of middle-class women within familial and domestic spaces. So also, often stories are made up about the woman theatre worker, and these transform her into a useful and attractive vehicle to carry the sexual and physical desires of society.

In the 1930s, as theatre began to transform into a new workplace, many women, especially from lower socio-economic backgrounds, began to take part in this workplace. The Savarna middle-class, which formed a large percentage of the theatre-going public, wanted to see their own cultural symbols and language reflected onstage and preferred actors who could fulfil that desire. And those who fulfilled these expectations of beauty and attractiveness, as well as the ability to speak what was seen as 'clean' or 'pure' Malayalam, were able to enjoy popularity and survived in this space for longer.

Commenting on this phenomenon, veteran actor Kuttyedathi Vilasini says: 'My real name is Brony, and I am the daughter of Joseph and Annamma from Iringalakkuda. It was the director of my first play, Kochuttanasan, who suggested that I change my name. "You won't survive the art world with this name," he told me. "It is ruled by Savarnas, Nairs, Hindus. They'll keep you at a distance." And that's how I became Vilasini, which then became Kozhikode Vilasini and Kuttyedathi Vilasini.'

This is not the isolated story of Brony from Iringalakkuda but is a path that many who came into this field took. Theatre workers come from a variety of caste, religious and economic backgrounds, and the respect they are shown may depend on their social circumstances, talent, luck, attractiveness, capability, and so on. But the woman theatre worker who participates in one or two shows every day, travels long distances, spends nights away from home, and shares the stage 'touching and acting' with other men—she has, throughout time, been called a 'loose woman', harlot, prostitute. Her life as an artist is a tightrope walk between admiration and condemnation, respect and ridicule.

The experiences revealed in my conversations with women actors, and in their own writings and memoirs, have, by and large, been set aside from the history of Malayalam theatre. My purpose here is to write them into history. Thus far, recorded history has been accepted—misunderstood—as simple truth. Charlotte Canning has suggested that women historians of the theatre looked to other methods because they were convinced that existing historiographic methods were insufficient in capturing women's experiences.[2] Women historians began to consider women's experiences as primary texts for writing history. 'Experience' denotes the process by which subjectivity is formed in a given context—a subjectivity that cannot be separated from the events, emotions and thoughts formed in that context. It is only through exposing and examining women's experiences that male-centred definitions of history and methods of writing history can be deconstructed, and in this process of deconstruction, women can re-examine their actions and identities. Even so, it must be remembered that one woman's experience is not the absolute truth about all women's experiences or the expression of all womanhood. Experiences are born of a self-awareness that disintegrates in discourses that are multi-layered and changeable. Still, historians such as Gerda Lerner consider experiential testimonies to be decisive.[3]

The Paths That Lead to a Life on Stage

Does the stage allow women to actualize their self-expression? The experiences of women actors seem to intimate that it does not and yet every woman who comes into this space tries to make it so despite, perhaps, being fully aware of it. Popular narratives quote economic deprivation as the most common factor that bring women to work in theatre. However, their own testimonies seem to trouble the singular meaning attributed, by society and sometimes by their own words, to economic factors, and address another common factor—the love for art. Still, as we shall see, it is difficult to attribute uniformity across the circumstances that brought them to the theatre.

'Being an actor was my biggest dream. At school, I took part in all kinds of cultural programmes. It was a close relative of ours that introduced me to the theatre.' (V.T. Stella, theatre, television and movie actor.)

'My husband left me, and I was stuck not knowing how to look after my kids. My involvement in theatre was the accidental result of trying to make a living.' (Sarojam S., professional theatre actor.)

'At first it was only about my interest in the art—then it became a way to make a living.' (Girija P., professional theatre actor.)

'An arts club in my village decided to put on a play. It had two women characters. They brought someone from outside to play one of the characters. They said I should play the other one, and in the end I agreed.' (Prabhavathi M., professional theatre actor.)

'The female actor left, and the samithi was in trouble, the play was almost certainly going to be cancelled. That's when my husband thought why not get me to do the part. He asked my opinion. Music and acting had always been two of my favourite subjects, so I didn't have to think twice to agree. And so, I became his heroine on stage just as I was in life!' (Thankam Vasudevan Nair, musician and actor.)

These personal testimonies suggest that their entry on to the stage was often accidental and unplanned and prompted by financial considerations. And yet, they also point to their artistic talents and aspirations, problematizing their own narratives. Other narratives add to this scenario. G. Omana, sister of the playwright and actor N.N. Pilllai, came to the stage acting in his play *Assalamu Alaikkum*. 'She was twenty-three then. The play, which called for solidarity between Hindus and Muslims, had a character who was the mother of the part played by Pillai himself. They tried several actors but none of them were suitable. And because the pay was measly, it was difficult finding someone to play the part on a long-term basis. So he looked to someone at home—his sister—and she agreed.'[4] Another award-winning actor, Savithri Sreedharan, was a dancer first, and had watched women actors such as Kuttyedathi Vilasini and Santhakumari with great interest when they came to act in the plays performed at the events where she danced. Married at sixteen, Savithri says that it was the encouragement and support from her husband and father that made her life on stage possible.

'My interest in acting was based on the fact that drama was the artform closest to life,' says Kuttyedathi Vilasini. She was a road construction worker when, encouraged by a dance teacher, she began to dance in a circus company, and later got into theatre and cinema. She went on to win several awards and continues to be an energetic presence in cinema and television.

'I knew some dance'; 'As a child, I loved singing and acting'; 'I've won many prizes at school'—such statements are strewn across the personal testimonies of women stage actors, indicating that while they explained their entry into theatre as 'accidental' or 'financially instigated', they chose theatre as their workplace because of their talents and interests. Several of these women had started their journeys acting in school plays or in amateur theatre before becoming professionals. Some were part of families already involved in artistic endeavours and were encouraged by fathers or brothers. A much smaller group came to this work after marriage and with the support of their husbands, while a majority have come to this path through playwrights, directors and brokers (agents). Many of Malayalam's leading literary and theatre figures—Thoppil Bhasi, P.K. Venukuttan Nair, C.G. Gopinath, Ponkunnam Varky, Ulloor Ramakrishnan, Nilambur Ayisha, Sudharma—have been instrumental in bringing them to this work.

The Theatre as Livelihood

The potential for making a living out of stage acting is dependent on several factors such as the success of the play and the duration and seasons of performance. There is no uniformity of pay within the field. For many women, earning enough to look after themselves and their families was an important consideration.

> 'No, what I make is not even enough to pay for my children's education. I still don't have a home of my own. Just struggling in the middle of all these debts.' (Sarojam S., came to the theatre after being abandoned by her husband.)

> 'The income from the theatre has helped my family survive as well as pay for my education.' (Binduraj, active participant in contemporary theatre.)

> 'Each year is dependent on the success of the play. Rainy season brings quite some difficulties.' (Cecily, permanent association with professional theatre company Kalaynilayam.)

> 'It is primarily my livelihood. It also allows me to show off my talents, interact with a variety of people, and sometimes it also helps me to forget my sorrows.' (Ramani, entered the theatre through dance and musical drama.)

A large number of actors I spoke with are of the opinion that a significant gendered gap exists in payscales with men being paid much more than women. Others also suggest that men and women who play the main roles are paid so much more than the supporting actors of both genders. The pay is also influenced by factors such as seniority, fame, perceived glamour and so on. My investigations also show that there is still a dearth of women coming into the theatre as actors, and because of this scarcity, women are comparatively better paid than in other fields.

Attesting to the fact that, for many women, the theatre is a crucial financial lifeline, an actor currently in her sixties says: 'It is with my income from acting on stage that I looked after my family, educated my younger sisters. No one acknowledges any of this, but they haven't forsaken me either probably because they accept that I have helped them. I came to this work at the age of thirteen. Even now, my family depends on my income. So I have not thought about resting or retirement.'

Experiences of not being paid by amateur theatre companies and festival organizers were common. 'I went to Thrissur to act in a play,' says Pattambi Subhadra, a professional actor who started her career acting in amateur theatre. 'Another actor, Velappaya Radha, was also with me. Radha's mother told me, insisted, that I ask for the payment before I put on the make-up. This was a new lesson. Another time, in Thrissur again, I did not ask for the payment before the show. When the show finished, the committee folk said they can't pay because they didn't have the money. Not even for my bus fare back. So I went to the house of the dignitary who had come to inaugurate the event the day before. And I got paid only because of his intervention.'

When they associate themselves with a troupe, they are obligated to do their work as stipulated in the contract. Withdrawing is not easy no matter how many negative experiences they might have to endure. If they do, they will then be deprived of a livelihood, and other companies would have finished their recruitment. Given this situation, and with the responsibility of looking after their families squarely on their shoulders, many women have learnt to demand their wages and actively challenge any attempts at being shortchanged. Pattam Saraswathiyamma, whose experiences with Sree Chithira Thirunal Granthasala we have discussed earlier, says: 'In those days, I was in all the plays, sometimes doing four plays at one time. And I asked for fifty rupees for each of these plays. Fifty rupees was a big deal for me in those days. And because my whole family had to survive on this, I would insist on being paid no matter what anyone said.'

'The main male actor was paid around sixty rupees,' recalls Aranmula Ponnamma. 'When they came and pressed me to join their drama, I said I wanted a hundred rupees per stage, and they promised to pay a hundred and one rupees. They were desperate, I suppose, and getting someone like me must have seemed a big deal to them.' Ponnamma, it must be remembered, was talking about a time when women were only beginning to enter the stage.

These sentiments are reflected in the memories of other actors, such as KPAC Sulochana and Sudharma. When Sulochana began her own theatre group, she did away with the custom of not paying actors for the sixth performance. (The money made from the sixth stage, as discussed earlier, went into the pockets of certain people involved under the pretext of being set aside for the party's welfare.) It was the memory, Sulochana says, of her own struggles to make ends meet and provide for her family that made her change this practice. An instance of the changes women's vision brought about within the theatre that are often overlooked.

Surviving Sexual Stereotyping

Even in the middle of the previous century, the practice of men impersonating women on stage continued, denoting the continuing scarcity of women in the field. The testimonies and memoirs of women actors make it clear that it was not the lack of talented women interested in the art that precipitated this situation, but the persisting negative social perception of stage acting.

'When I came to acting, what motivated me more than my interest in the art was the possibility of getting out of financial uncertainty,' recalls Iringal Narayani. 'It was my uncle who led the way. I began with the play *Kanchana*, which was staged in Iringal in 1952. It was a time when women were not brave enough to come into the field, and I, who'd jumped right in, became an irritation in the eyes of the community. And the result was ostracization that went on for seven long years!' She goes on to say that this experience of being ostracized by her community was also what drove her to continue acting both on stage and in cinema. And true to her resolve, she acted in over 300 plays and ten or so movies, and made a name as drama music director.

Many such experiences of scorn, rejection and contempt exist in the memories of these actors.

'In the beginning, people looked at me as though I was immoral. I suffered a lot . . .'

'They had such a low view of us. That hasn't changed much even now. Due to this I had given up acting, but then had to come back after a while because of the situation at home.'

'People had so much misunderstanding. They thought going to work in the night and acting in plays were bad.'

'When I went to my work and while coming back with clear signs of sleep deprivation and exhaustion—people would sneer at me and laugh scornfully right at my face.'

> 'People considered acting as a ruse to make more money through prostitution.'

> 'To tell you in simple Malayalam—"veshya", prostitute. Even now that viewpoint exists, except that there is a bit of change because there is a section of people who respect the profession.'

In the early days of women's participation in theatre, people were not ready to show them the respect and appreciation, however limited, that they had for dancers and musicians. 'Progressives objected, reactionaries showered blame'—this sentiment recurs in the memories of women actors. These attitudes are not entirely a thing of the past either. 'Even now, people in rural areas think that only bad women went to act in plays,' said a woman actor. 'I used to go for dance programmes initially, which didn't create many problems. But when I started acting on stage, relatives and neighbours began to object. So much trouble they made when my colleagues came home to invite me to act in plays—even now this situation hasn't changed. I just don't listen to any of it.'

The isolation women experienced because of these responses is evident in the following testimonies:

> 'When I go to worship in the church, I sit at the back. I can't help feeling that everyone is looking at me as though I was an accused, and I want to withdraw into myself.'

'I ran into an old friend of mine on a bus, and with great joy I took her child and placed her on my lap. She snatched the child off me and went and sat in a seat away from me. Like I was a leper or had some communicable disease.'

The veteran actor KPAC Beatrice has much to say about these experiences. Born in 1938, she became famous after acting, at the age of thirteen, in P.J. Antony's *Charitharthyam*. She was associated with KPAC and was acting in their production of *Puthiya Akasham, Puthiya Bhoomi* when she began to receive marriage proposals. The leaders of her community saw to it that none of these proposals came to fruition. Finally, she had to atone for her 'sin' by carrying a cross at the church during Qurbana. 'The five-o-clock worship was attended only by a few people,' she recalls. 'I went into the church, took a wooden cross and stood there carrying it until it ended.' The church relented and gave her permission to marry, but it was a long time before she actually found a husband. Following the marriage, she left the stage for a long while, and returned to acting after the death of her husband when there was no other way to look after her family and her two children.

Adoor Pankajam, one of Kerala's most venerated senior artists, also recalls similar experiences. When she came home after acting in her first play, her neighbours and relatives looked upon her as though she was tainted. Her grandmother told her, 'back from whoring around? Do not enter this house without bathing and purifying yourself.' She recalls that only her father stood by her. Pankajam also attests that at least early/older actors like her can expect courtesy and respect these days. "'No play today?' neighbours enquire fondly, and women too say, proudly, "I have a stage today."' She finds this shift in attitude most satisfying.

It is also this shift in perception that saw actor Savithri Sreedharan elected as the corporation councillor in Manari in Kozhikode, an acknowledgement also of her identity as an actor. Still, when an actor proudly makes the statement, 'no one called me a stage actor,' it points to the multiple meanings attributed to this identity. This is reflected in how actors feel about their own daughters entering the field. Some say that their daughters are not interested in the field, not even in their mothers' involvement, while others are reluctant to lead their daughters into the field even when they are talented. 'We know what we have suffered,' they say in explanation.

At the same time, there are women who are proud that their daughters have followed in their footsteps. 'This is the field they have grown up watching,' says one actor. 'When they were looking for someone to fulfil the role of a child, I took my daughter. Now she acts in amateur theatre while also getting on with her education.'

The views of a new generation of women who are currently entering the field and making it their own provide hope for the future. 'I always wanted to come into the field, having grown up watching my mother and going to many drama camps,' says one actor. 'I know this field very well and regard it with great respect. And I make enough to pay for my education.'

Rani, who holds a law degree, has had to hear certain unsavoury comments from her friends who got to know that she was also a theatre actor. Still, she hopes to continue acting even after she takes on a job as a lawyer. Swathi is the daughter of actors Jaya and Naushad, both of whom are proud of her work as an actor. 'How long can you hide your talent?' asks Jaya who came into the field from a rural village and had experienced financial troubles as well as personal attacks.

Participating as a worker within the space of the theatre is, as has been demonstrated, at once joyful and saddening. Many of these women find not having the opportunity to express their talents difficult. At the same time, living life as a theatre artist in the wider community is challenging. And when these challenges become unbearable, many of them also find it hard to leave because they often have responsibilities towards their families that they cannot shirk. It is this conflict that emerges most forcefully in their testimonies.

Inside the Company

Discussions about the difficulties women encounter when trying to mark out their own space on the male-dominated stage are widespread within contemporary Malayalam theatre. Each woman actor entering this space has to contend with patriarchal moral codes that govern the space. As a slice of society, the stage imposes upon the woman actor a set of rules based in these moral codes while simultaneously subjecting her to its immoral gaze, rule-breaking and obscenities. The movement of the female body on stage and in the mind of the audience is codified in a way that satisfies furtive male glances; her body language expected to sustain the patriarchal moral structure while also providing fulfilment to the male gaze.

In the course of my conversations with women actors, I asked them two questions: 1) Did they experience negative behaviour from their colleagues, members of their drama companies? 2) Did they experience negative and hurtful behaviour from company owners, directors, main actors and brokers, essentially people in positions of power within a company? Both these questions were answered either in one word—'Yes'—or with the sentence, 'too many to recount'. Not many people were willing to talk specifics or identify the companies or persons involved. The perpetrators of sexual harassment were often company owners, directors, writers and main actors, as well as brokers who offer to help actors find placements in drama troupes in exchange for sexual favours. The overwhelming reticence in answering these questions points to the helplessness of these women, who are unable to challenge and survive such situations. As one actor put it, 'too bitter to swallow, too sweet to spit out—that, in essence, is my life as an actor.' Many were of the opinion that the only thing they could do was physical resistance, which invariably led to character assassination:

> The play ended, and we all went back to the camp. Those who lived nearby and those who could travel back home left. The only people left were me and the man who was in charge of the troupe. He brought me a cup

of coffee, tapped me lightly on my shoulder and stepped out. I was about to shut the door when he pushed it back trying to get in the room. I pushed back with all my might. There we were, on either side of the door, but I could see that I won't be able to stand up to his strength too long. So he pushed in and I let go and he fell into the room. I ran out. It was five-thirty in the morning. It is not that safe to be standing alone at a bus stop at that time, but what to do when it was equally dangerous inside and outside.

This incident, described to me in a written response strewn with spelling mistakes, points to the complexities in the world of these women and to the many stories hidden behind every cryptic 'yes' I received as responses to the questions I posed. Even where there is no physical attack, women have to put up with innuendos and gossip that ruin their reputation and their dignity, as exemplified in the following excerpt:

There is an artist in our troupe. He loves making up stories connecting women to some man or the other. He began a rumour about me and a colleague who I loved and interacted with like my own brother. Then it escalated to sending us anonymous letters wanting to cause trouble between us. All I can say is that god will punish such gossips who embarrass women and ruin their future.

A famous actor took me into the exploitative world that exists behind the curtains in today's theatre world:

You don't know the dramas inside dramas. The troupe owner is expected to provide alcohol to the agents. But not just alcohol in some cases, they also expect that a woman actor is served up to them too. I am a woman; I am never ever going to do that. And so, my troupe's play did not get many bookings to perform on many stages.

Meanwhile, there are also actors who have only had positive and joyful experiences of being involved with drama troupes. Pattambi Subhadra, for instance, says that the theatre as a workplace has fewer problems compared to what women have to endure in other workplaces. 'I got a temporary position at the panchayat office via the employment exchange,' she recalls. 'But when it was time for the position to be made permanent, I was told I had to "satisfy" a certain man. I wouldn't do that, so I had to resign. I find that the theatre is a good field for women. Without a woman actor, a play won't happen. She has that position and power in her group.'

As with other workplaces, anti-women behaviour from colleagues is a reality in this space too. A stage actor's work environment (rehearsal camps, travel to performances, accommodation) is outside the home, involves evenings and nights, and is often in the company of men. Women who inhabit public spaces in the night cause anxieties for the society's moral fabric, and so the morality of every woman who makes the decision to participate in this work environment is under constant surveillance and questioning, not only by the society but also by her colleagues in that same work environment. The violence aimed at her body and mind arises from the twisted idea that women in public spaces do not have the right to privacy. The world of the theatre is full of such conflicts even as there exists, within the same space, healthy, enabling relationships.

Testimonies of married women, especially whose husbands are also actors, reveal another element of how women are treated within this workplace. Actors who are involved in the same drama troupes as their husbands or within the circle of their acquaintances said that they had never experienced negative behaviours within these circles.

> 'I was twenty when I started acting. After six years in the field, I married a person who I had met in the field. I continued in the professional troupe until 1991, and in all that time, I have never had any trouble.'

> 'I believe that I have not faced any problems because I had my husband's label attached to me. It has come in quite handy.'

The other side of this feeling of safety is the fact of exploitation with the promise of marriage and family. Believing in the promise of marriage from a company owner, one woman had provided her acting services without pay during the initial, difficult years of the troupe, only to be driven away when the troupe became successful. In the interviews I conducted, several women alluded to the practice of company owners keeping women actors as temporary wives in order to ensure that they did not look for other opportunities. 'My son's father is a drama samithi owner who has a wife and children of his own,' said one woman after seeking the strictest anonymity. 'He was supportive in my direst need and sorrow, but now I and my son have no one to depend on.' Women were not reluctant to blame their co-workers who found themselves in these situations, in effect pointing to the common tendency to put the onus of discipline and morality on women themselves: 'We shouldn't lose our mind. We should have the ability to know what's what at least by the time we are fifteen. Don't lose your caution, and if something untoward happens, show the courage to leave. We're not anyone's chattel.'

Even within well-known, progressive theatre companies, there are different disciplinary rules for men and women. Under the guise of protecting women, several practices exist: opening the letters addressed to women actors before handing them over; not allowing visitors or only allowing five minutes with them; not letting them go out on their own; allowing them out only in the company of troupe members acting as chaperones; making them have their meals in their rooms. Companies take all these measures in the name of women's safety instead of creating safer work environments. Sexual exploitation of women workers happens in all workplaces, but there is a prevailing feeling among women actors of the stage that they are mentally and economically weak and unsafe, which makes it harder to respond to and challenge this exploitation. The fact that there is no job security or benefits other than their wages makes their situation precarious. Those with responsibilities of bringing up children find themselves more reluctant to speak out than others.

Experiencing the Workplace as a Collective

One of the important themes I explored in my conversations with women actors was their experiences of satisfaction and happiness in relation with their work and workplace. What joyful moments did drama give the women who had dedicated their lives to it? Much of the responses to this query were in terms of winning awards or accolades, including those from the audience. Although I was hoping to hear about joyful moments in working within a collective and the satisfaction gained from it, there were barely any responses along those lines. Some testimonies throw light on why this was so. 'I don't even know if there is much of a collective in the professional theatre field,' one woman told me. 'Most companies I know tend to keep women actors separate and isolated. The men in the troupe get together but the fact is that they don't involve women in discussions or analyses about the play or its reception.'

Comments were also made that these gatherings of men often involved consuming alcohol, and that these sessions would often disintegrate into arguments and altercations. According to actors with experiences of working in amateur as well as professional fields, opportunities to be a genuine part of a collective were more likely to be in the amateur theatre circuit.

Fonder memories of collectives and coming together were more to be found in the reminiscences of actors from an earlier era. KPAC Sulochana, Kozhikode Elsy, Savithri Sreedharan, Kuttyedathi Vilasini and Vijayakumari

(Kalidasa Kalakendram) recalled such experiences with obvious joy. They complained that there had been an erosion of mutual respect in the field that they see as highly commercialized. Elsy Sukumaran, who was born in 1953 and began acting at the age of twelve, says, 'even the nomenclature "sangamam" (coming together) of drama troupes came out of the fact that it was an actual coming together of people of different castes and backgrounds. Each long-distance journey was a joyful occasion, singing songs all through the night. When things got busy during performances, we would all pitch in to put the curtains up and arrange the sets and so on. No one pushed us aside because we were women. I don't see that mutual respect anymore; it is all a business.'

Theatre work, by definition, is a collaborative effort, so the insider view from the field of professional theatre that women in these collectives are seen only as actors and not also as collaborators is dispiriting. Other than receiving an award or recognition, all that is left of happy memories are travels and visits to temples. The most cherished memories, for the very few who had this opportunity, were about sitting together discussing the successes and failures after performances.

The Show Must Go On

One of the saddest facts of professional theatre is that no matter what calamity befalls, the show that has been booked in advance must go on. The practice of having an understudy, ready and trained to step in during an emergency does not exist within the entire history of professional theatre in Kerala. Women actors have several distressing stories about being caught within this situation, and most of these were of loss—of deaths that occurred on stage; of keeping the news of the death of a loved one from actors until the end of the long tour; of losing friends while on tour; of accidents while rushing desperately from one venue to another. These stories also reveal the depth of their dedication to their chosen field of work and to the mission of progressive theatre.

'I had two small children, and my husband was very unwell and there was no one else to look after him,' says a famous actor recounting her experiences. 'The play was fully booked. When the company was in financial difficulties, we would often help out by doing more than one role. But when we have a need, they won't reciprocate. How I suffered in those days.' Another actor, Meena Ganesh, who became famous as a director as well as in the fields of cinema and television, recalls her experience: 'They called to say there was a performance the next day. I set out early from Shoranur and got to Alappuzha by noon. Suddenly, a hartal was called by a political party and there were no buses going south. Vehicles of other drama troupes were passing by and I tried to hitch a ride, but none of them stopped. I ran after one for a while, and finally they stopped, perhaps feeling sorry for me. I was so tired and hungry by this time.' One time, the drama troupe's vehicle got in an accident. Afraid that if she went to the hospital, she might be admitted, Meena took painkillers and continued performing, resting in between scenes on a mat spread on the floor behind the stage. These are stories that indicate that those who worked in the field tried their best not to halt performances.

KPAC Sulochana talks about the death of her brother: 'I was about to go to a show in Kannur when he died suddenly. Everyone, including my colleagues and relatives, said the show should be cancelled. But I refused. I was too concerned about the financial and mental, and perhaps even physical, consequences for those who had booked our show and the bad name it would bring to our troupe if it was cancelled, and the financial difficulties for my co-actors. So I waited until the final rites were done and then went to Kannur in a van with my nephew.'[5]

The famous actor Balusseri Sarasa remembers continuing with the play after falling off the stage during a performance and breaking her arm. She continued acting with the broken arm throughout that season. 'I wasn't sure how I would live for the rest of the year if I left the show. So I persevered despite the pain and discomfort. When an artist, man or woman, became unwell, not many people come to their aid.'

Looking at these experiences, one might think that all women, especially those who work in the private sector, face similar situations. It must be stressed, however, that the theatre is a different workplace. The work lasts only for a few months of the year—'the season'—and the only way to make the play a success is to perform on as many stages as possible during that time. One person's absence adversely affects not only themselves but a whole wider community including other members of the troupe, the company owner, the organizers who book performances, as well as the audience. This places a huge responsibility on the shoulders of actors.

The other major factor is financial. A day's work lost is a day's wages lost, not only for the person but for the other members of the group. The more they are booked, the more they travel, the more the wages. There is no sick leave to apply for, no time off.

Travels, Travails

Perhaps one of the most distressful elements of professional theatre for women actors is the long journeys they have to endure. It is in the nature of professional theatre in Kerala that most performances are not in city auditoriums but in festival grounds in villages. A drama troupe often has to travel along country roads without even the primary facilities. The fact that, even today, Kerala's public space fails to provide women with the bare minimum amenities makes this even more complex. The vehicles they travel in are often unsuitable for long distances and are overcrowded. Women are more often than not relegated to the back seats where they endure the discomfort of the vehicle navigating unmaintained, potholed roads. Women seemed resigned to the discomfort of travel as though accepting it as an inherent part of being women. Even stopping for a comfort break is something they have to negotiate themselves. 'The troupe don't care,' said one respondent. 'We ask the manager to stop the vehicle in front of some house along the way, and we get out and ask the householders to let us use their toilet.'

Talking to me on the television documentary *Penmalayalam*, KPAC Sulochana remembered: 'We sit there holding it in, sometimes for hours, either because we are reluctant to ask or because we know there are no facilities that we could use. Can't use dirty toilets with no water! Sometimes it would be so bad that it would affect my health and I wouldn't be able to sing. I've had to go to doctors in a few places.' Kuttyedathi Vilasini has had similar experiences. 'Most troupes relegate women to the back seats in the vehicle. By the time you come back after a trip, your body is in pain. And when we have our periods, it's truly hard. We've had to get our basic needs done behind bushes screening each other with our bodies or behind a cloth tied as a screen in the greenroom.'

The world of theatre is understood as a man's world, and women, who are fewer in number, tend not to voice their needs. The secrecy and silence around women's bodies forbid them from talking about bodily needs in public. Women, too, share in the idea that natural female phenomena such as menstruation is something disgusting, never to be talked about or handled, and so many actors are unable to even admit the basic needs surrounding their body. Meanwhile, company owners and members have a general attitude of carelessness and irresponsibility when it comes to women's bodily needs. What is not addressed is the fact that the body—its health, energy and physicality—is an inseparable part of the work that they do; it is the primary tool that actors employ. Women's testimonies underline the fact that this field, more than any other, needs to address how to facilitate care and compassion when it comes to basic bodily needs.

After the travails of these journeys, when they get to the venues, more often than not in festival grounds in the countryside, everyone looks forward to a little rest before the performance and hopes that the organizers have set a place aside for this. Almost always, this will be at a house near the festival ground. Delving into how the women in these households treated actors is revealing.

Many have overheard scornful comments, 'Oh, those "acting women" are here!' Sometimes, the organizers take actors to a house without prior arrangement only to have the doors shut in their faces. Some refuse to let them into the house, instead spreading a few mats outside in the yard. 'It hurt me deeply,' wrote an actor in her response, 'to experience this after having travelled such a long distance.' Another actor, who had been in the field for over fifteen years, recalled: 'We went to Gudalur for a programme where our rest was arranged in the house of a prominent person in the community. As soon as we entered, the women of the household went inside and shut the doors.' Another woman said, 'they sat looking at us as though we were dolls in a display case.'

Faced with such negative reactions, many women go back to their vehicles and wait it out until it is time to get ready for the performance. Overall, most women expressed the feeling that as women actors, this was their fate and they just had to live with it.

If this was the story of life on the road, what of drama camps? Only a handful of established companies like KPAC or Kalidasa Kalakendram have permanent rehearsal camps with facilities. Most other companies have one-room camps.

A famous actor testifies: 'I joined a group in northern Kerala because of financial issues. The pay in Malabar is usually less than what we are used to in the south. When I agreed, they had shown me the respect that came with my fame, but when I began working with them, the company owner began showing his real side. The camp was a house, dirty and unkempt. There were beedi and cigarette stubs everywhere. No furniture, chairs, tables, beds, nothing. The toilet was a hole in the ground. The other women said nothing. They put up with everything in order to honour their word!'

My conversations with actors showed that there were serious issues to be addressed in this context, but few were willing to come out and discuss what they were, confining, instead, their answers to one-liners—'Ah, that's all a long story!' or 'what to do other than put up with it!' The only ray of hope in the scenario is that there are a handful of troupes that provide basic amenities.

The Eye of the Beholder

All art depends on audience response; each artist desires that their art is well received by its audience. Being a good audience member is as difficult as being a good artist. Just as a play finds its audience, an audience defines the art that is drama. The major part in this process of defining art by its audience, even today, is undertaken by men, and so it is through their gaze that the conditions of women's bodies and their movements on stage are established. As we have already seen, Ochira Velukkutty became famous as a female impersonator in the 1930s because he could satisfy the male audience. This male audience did not care whether the actor on stage was a man or a woman as long as their movements, methods and motifs satisfied their expectations. This fact is evidenced by how, towards the end of the 1940s, when women came to the stage in considerable numbers, Velukkutty continued to shine in the role of Vasavadatta in the play *Karuna*. 'The roles of Vasavadatta's handmaids were all apprised by real women and yet this actor, with his unparalleled skill, outshone all of them,' writes the playwright C.L. Jose. 'With little obvious effort, he performed Vasavadatta's lust-filled glances, gestures and expressions in a way that only the most gifted of women actors could accomplish.'[6]

A.M. Agasthamma (Thankamma), who played the role of a handmaid in the play, remembers the experience. 'Velukkutty had diabetes. The plan was to perform *Karuna* and pay for his treatment with the money. I still remember the performance at Thrissur High School. Velukkutty, of course, was Vasavadatta. Papputti Bhagavathar and Mavelikkara Ponnamma were also there. Backstage, I saw this stunningly beautiful woman with thick, long hair flowing down her back. Who is that, I asked, and Mavelikkara Ponnamma said, that is the great Velukkutty bhagavathar.' Agasthamma donated her wages from the play for his treatment.

The woman figure that Velukkutty embodied—appreciated equally onstage and offstage—was shaped in a way that fulfilled the desire of the male gaze. It is only when this desire is satisfied that the audience embraces the character. For women actors, there is the keenly felt discomfort of being the object of the audience's sexual desire even before she embodies her character onstage. This discomfort was voiced in several different ways in our conversations, including having to put up with accusatory looks, drunken advances, obscene comments, expressed disgust and behaviour that made them feel they were strange creatures who were not part of society.

Despite this scenario, in a context where drama troupes gave a great deal of consideration to star value and fan following, audience appreciation is a blessing to women actors. Early actors, especially those who were part of the progressive theatre, have written about audience appreciation and the respect they had enjoyed. KPAC Sulochana records that she had been overwhelmed with the love from her audience: 'A bunch of people came from the leprosy hospital to see the play, *Ashwamedham*. After the performance, they came and hugged me, and sobbed that I was their sister. That was a moving experience.'[7]

Maxim Gorky's *Mother* was presented in Malayalam for the first time by Kozhikode Ranachethana, which was part of the Janakeeya Samskarikavedi formed during 1977–78. The role of the mother was performed by the actor Stella, with Joy Mathew in the role of the son, Pavel. 'At every stage, after the performance, audience members came backstage and expressed their appreciation,' remembers Stella, who is still active in the fields of cinema, television and dubbing. 'You are our own mother, they would say, and put red garlands around my neck.'

Most of the negative experiences were in the form of unwanted and unacceptable comments made, including while on stage. Exploring this issue revealed several such incidents:

> 'Often, they would sit right at the front and pass obscene comments as though we were not even human. These are distracting, and there have been times when the curtain had to be downed and the play stopped.'

> 'It is women actors who have to endure these comments, including graphic descriptions of our bodies. There's only so much we can put up with.'

> 'It doesn't matter what they come up with, we have to finish the performance, don't we? So, we endure. I try not to pay attention to them, but I'm not deaf, am I?'

> 'Some comments make me shiver and my heart beats as though it is about to burst.'

> 'They say things, and if we pay attention to it, we forget our lines.'

> 'Sometimes we are so tired and sleep-deprived that we might miss a line or so, and if that happens, terrible obscenities are hurled at us. Some men even expose themselves.'

Obscene comments from the audience are aimed at the woman who is the actor and not at the role she plays. Contemporary actors' comments add another dimension to this. Those who play negative characters involving cheating or deception, or those who have to portray their characters dressed in modern clothes, have to endure more of this type of behaviour. Heckling is part of the theatre experience, but women are subjected to this more than men. Sitting in the front rows, making drunken and obscene comments and exposing themselves, these male audience members affect the work of women actors and make their workplace complex and dangerous. The situation is not a modern one; it existed in the early years of women's engagement with theatre. Writing in his memoir *Ezhayiram Ravukal*, actor Thoppil Krishnapilla says, 'a large number of contractors who book performances for festivals were gundas. They refuse to hand over the agreed fee after the performance. There have been instances where they have held women actors ransom.'[8]

These instances underline the risk that women in those days took in order to be part of the theatre. Alappuzha Ammini (the stage name of Philomena, who has acted in over 500 plays) was an actor who travelled to performances without a companion, and this incident is one that she remembers with fear:

> We went for a performance in Pala. There were two of us women, me and the actor Chellamma. We were young and pretty in those days. Some folk, rich money bags, had conspired with the sound-and-light technicians to abduct us. The plan was that, as soon as the final curtain fell, they would switch off all the lights and capture us. Thankfully, the light technician was a

good man, and he told us about this plan. So with the help of M.N. Kuruvila Sir, who was the one who invited us to perform, as soon as the play was over, we ran out and through a sugarcane field until we reached the road.

Others have had to face even more dangerous situations. Perhaps one of the most notorious of these incidents was the attempt on Nilambur Ayisha's life when she was on stage while acting in *JJu Nalloru Mansanakan Nokku*. 'We were performing at Melakkam in Manjeri,' she writes in her memoir. Everything was going on smoothly when, suddenly, a shot was fired at me. It was sheer luck that I was delivering my dialogue while pacing the stage. It was not that the person who fired the gun missed, just that I had moved. The bullet passed exactly where I was a moment earlier and pierced the back curtain. It was a calculated act to harm me.'[9]

The workplace of the theatre is riddled with complexities. The discomfort arising from women's presence on stage, and the responses from audience members are all aimed primarily at the women who occupy this space. The community of audience that changes over time is what decides the language of the theatre as well as its successes or failures. Theatre as a means of livelihood is heavily dependent on the success of the performances, and because of this, women actors have no other option than to confront the desires of the audience both within the language of the theatre as well as in its outward, physical manifestation.

Behind the Scenes

Every student of drama learns about the importance of backstage preparations needed to transform into their characters, including the calm and peace required when putting on the costume and make-up. How do women experience this space as they prepare for the stage?

'They stand outside the greenroom and talk dirty,' says one actor. 'Often these greenrooms are temporary structures made of plaited palm leaves, which we then cover on the inside with cloth (to stop Peeping Toms). There have been instances when the cloth has been cut through with razor blades. They seem to believe that they have the right to a full view of the woman's body that is on stage.'

This situation existed even when men impersonated women on stage, as is evident from Ochira Velukkuty's experience. 'Lecherous audience members, infatuated with his female roles, would peep through the screens as he took off his costume,' writes Sebastian Kunjukunju Bhagavathar.[10] This situation caused great distress to Velukkutty, to the extent that there have been times when he had to take off his clothes to prove that he was a man. Writing about his experiences while with KPAC, Thoppil Krishnapilla records that the behaviour of the audience towards women actors can be even more problematic where the play garnered opposition. 'Women suffer more in these situations. Peeping Toms tear open the screens to ogle at them as they put on their make-up, call out obscenities. We try our best to protect them under these circumstances.'[11]

All women actors expect the sudden and unexpected intrusion of lustful gazes through the palm leaf/cloth screens that form their greenrooms and they exercise extreme caution, supporting and keeping watch over one another. A woman endures a range of barriers and ridicule in order to come to the workplace of the theatre, and when she does enter this workplace, she upsets the moral values of patriarchy. Society assumes that such a woman does not have the right to privacy, creating a situation where she is subjected to more attacks than she would face in any other field. To a limited extend they are able to stand up to the objectification and attacks they suffer as a result. However, if women actors are to feel safe, if theatre is to change into a space that does not allow anyone to destroy their identity, there has to be a concerted, collective sociopolitical intervention.

Why Do They Need Special Treatment?

'When I was acting in the play *Sthree*, I became pregnant. There were no stand-ins, so I had to continue acting. One day, by accident, I fell into a muddy hole. I couldn't climb out, couldn't move. My colleagues pulled me out somehow or the other but by then I was unconscious. There were no doctors anywhere nearby. They gave me first aid and I regained consciousness, but I was in such terrible pain. By then, it was past evening and time for the play. They couldn't easily cancel it, and I was adamant that it went ahead. So I sat there in severe pain while someone put the make-up on me. Before every scene, they carried me onstage, and I acted my entire part sitting down. After each scene I'd lay down and rest. Somehow, I got through the performance. And there were so many such experiences.

On the forty-first day after giving birth to my daughter Manimol, I was travelling to Chavara to act in the play, *Swarajyam*. The driver of the car was drunk and drove it into a fence. My child and I had to be pulled out of the crushed car. Thankfully, the child was unhurt, not even a scratch, but my chest sustained injuries. Breast milk and blood poured out. By then, the news that I was dead spread around Chavara. And when we finally reached there in a bullock cart, people had gathered wanting to view my dead body! In this instance too, I was adamant that the play was not cancelled, and I went ahead with my part. Every now and then, my chest needed to be cleaned off the milk and blood.'[12]

This story is narrated by Mavelikkara Ponnamma, one of the most popular and influential actors of early theatre. It resonates with women actors throughout history in relation to their experiences of dealing with the complexities and conflicts around pregnancy and breastfeeding. Women's physical needs in relation to reproduction have mental and emotional consequences. While these have developed in service to her natural role, they are also used as tools to control and confine her. In terms of her role within the theatre that is her workplace, these bodily factors can cause great distress which she may be reluctant to share with her male colleagues. The primary reason for this reluctance is the socialization that instructs her to keep these things secret. Specific issues that they face as they continue to be involved in theatre while menstruating, pregnant, breastfeeding, and so on are discussed here.

'I've had to endure so much discomfort during my periods. For instance, I was part of a group based in Thiruvananthapuram. The performance was in Thrissur, and I sat there the whole way without even being able to go to the bathroom. And then, after dancing on the stage, back to Thiruvananthapuram. I don't even want to think about those days!'

'When I have my periods, my performance is affected. There have been times when the periods have started while I was on stage. I can't describe that feeling. It is so hard to forget about the bodily discomfort and pain and focus only on the acting.'

Drama troupes are organized around the needs and conveniences of the men involved in them and often make no preparations for women's needs. Long journeys while menstruating, sitting in the backseats of vehicles bearing the pain and soaked in blood, the lack of clean toilet facilities with running water, dirty environments that cause infections—all of this becomes a routine part of the life and work of a woman actor. Given that society still maintains the archaic view that a menstruating body is unclean and untouchable, it creates an almost unbearable work environment even as a healthy body and mind are of extreme importance in doing their work well. The support and care from colleagues become crucial in these situations.

Society's attitudes about the cleanliness and purity of menstruating bodies also create extreme angst in some women when the performance is in grounds adjacent to temples. 'Sometimes, our rest will be arranged in the oottupura (the kitchen and dining area) of temples. On days of menstruation, I apologize to God—what else can I do?' said one actor. They try hard not to show their distress and focus on finishing their performances as best as they can.

Equally distressful are the days when they go to work while pregnant or when breastfeeding. Women in this field depend on their physical abilities and movements more than in many other professions and it makes these periods more problematic for them.

> 'If we are pregnant, we just put up with all the associated difficulties and get on with the job of acting. Why, because we have to live! The owner of our troupe or our colleagues don't want to know. Breastfeeding mothers bring their babies along if they don't have anyone else to look after them, leave them in a cloth cradle temporarily hung in the greenroom, and leave them to the care of their co-workers when they are on stage.' (Alice Paul, professional theatre actor.)

> 'When I was pregnant, I continued acting in KPAC until I was seven months gone. Struggling for breath while acting with my belly bound tightly. One time, I put up with bleeding that went on for two months and continued acting, my body and tongue tired, yet focusing on giving the best performance I can.' (Pushpalatha, dancer and professional theatre actor.)

> 'I was hospitalized towards the end of my pregnancy. On the third day, I was discharged and went straight

to my job. On the eleventh day, I finally gave birth, and by the twenty-fifth day after that I was back on stage.' (Radhamaniyamma, professional theatre actor.)

'I was a singer with the Kalanilayam group for twelve years. I sang for two shows on the day I gave birth to my son—my contractions started as I was returning to the room after a song. On occasion, I have quietly slid behind the stage, breastfed my crying baby and gone back up even as the show went on.' (Kalanilayam Santha, professional theatre actor.)

'Going to act in theatre was not like it is nowadays. The travel to performances was hard work. When my son Satyajit was a baby, I would take him along with me, leave him in a cradle in the greenroom and go on stage. Sometimes, as I am doing a scene, I would hear him cry, but I would continue acting with an aching heart.' (Santhadevi, theatre and movie actor.)

These real-life experiences of women actors have always remained outside the accepted parameters of history writing. Theatre history has to rethink its methods and create a new way of writing history that encompasses these experiences.

She, My Friend

As we go through the experiences of women actors, one cannot escape the feeling of loneliness that each of them expressed. And yet, the accounts that they shared with me contained several descriptions of women's friendship and camaraderie, and remembrances of the good times spent together, about the difficulties others had experienced, and about stage acting in general. These accounts were also helpful in gathering information about actors from another era not found in history books.

One such example is that of Kozhikode Padmavathi, an influential actor at one time, and her important role in supporting other actors enter the field. 'Kozhikode Padmavathi was an excellent actor. She was the one who brought me into theatre,' remembers P. Vijayalakshmi, an active presence in the theatre world in Kozhikode, and the wife of the well-known actor Nilambur Balan. 'The money she placed in my hand as an advance turned into my livelihood for the rest of my life.' Vijayalakshmi recalls that towards the end of her life, Padmavathi had to live in penury: 'She hurt her leg in a road accident and became unable to walk without help. She was the wife of a man in the same field, but in the end, she was alone except for her son, her only child. Before she died, she sent word that she wanted to see me. We sat together, remembering and retelling old stories. She said she needed an operation to set her leg right and asked for help. I said I will see what I can do. She was hoping that she could go back to acting or take up some other job once her leg was fixed. But the next thing I heard was the news of her death. They say it was suicide.'

Friendship and support between women within the space of the theatre were crucial for many women in how they experienced and survived the space. Many recalled instances of cooperation and practical support. In her memoir about her personal experiences, KPAC Sulochana recalls several such instances: 'When we were involved in the production of *Puthiya Akasham Puthiya Bhoomi*, the couple O. Madhavan and Vijayakumari had a child. We all called him Joymon (the famous Malayalam film actor Mukesh). They would bring him along to performances, and he would be in a cradle near the women's greenroom. We would all take turns to rock him and look after him. I remember singing to him during my breaks.'[13]

KPAC Lalitha, one of the most famous actors of Malayalam cinema and theatre, describes the relationship between women actors in the company as a family. 'Me, Sulochana, Rajamma, Beatrice, Sudharma, Leela, Krishnakumari ... we had such a strong relationship with each other. Every year in the month of Mithunam, when the season comes to an end, we would part with great sorrow. And until I was back with them at camp the next year, I would feel such a sense of loneliness.'

While there are several such stories about the friendship between women actors, there was also a simultaneous feeling that these friendships are hard to come by. Each person seems to live in a separate islet, with isolation as the shared common theme. So too, their reminiscences of the experiences of actors from an earlier era are felt as deeply as though they were instances from their own lives.

Anxieties about old age that is to come are also hidden in many of these reminiscences. There are, even today, actors whose families are dependent solely on their income. What would happen when they can no longer work? How would their lives go forward? 'Such is the fate of an actor's life,' many said, their words thick with helplessness. They were united in their opinion that the pension that retired, destitute actors receive (Rs 1,600 at the time of writing) is of no value other than as recognition of their contributions to society. Their experiences attest to the fact that, at the dusk of lives spent entertaining others through their creative talents, they are resigned to facing uncertainty and unhappiness.

All That Exists Between Women and Creativity

The testimonies of women actors discussed so far point to their work in a field that is predominantly distressful, difficult and demotivating. Why, then, continue in this field? Actors' responses to this question pointed to the value they placed on the theatre as the arena where they could express their creative talents.

'There was no one to look after the kids, and anyway no one here was interested in my acting, so I had to give up the stage,' says a retired actor. 'I can't tell you how it suffocates me, not being able to be on stage. And when I see drama troupe vehicles passing by on the road in front of my house, my heart breaks.' These words express her intense desire to perform on stage that she still nurtures even though she now has no financial worries. The opportunity to inhabit other personas, to experiment with the different facets of womanhood, to discover the well of human expressions hidden in her own psyche—these are the pleasures acting brought her.

The desire to explore their own individuality is an important part of their interest in this work. These are actors exceptionally capable of expressing the varied manifestations of womanhood created within patriarchal ideology. They are also fully aware of the gendered nature of performance, not only on stage but in their roles as wives, sisters, daughters and mothers with the ambition and talent to be actors.

'My favourite role was in C.N. Sreekantan Nair's play *Nashtakkachavatam*. I used to shine in the scene where I had to snatch my thali off and throw it away. No one gave me a life...' When the celebrated actor Pattam Saraswathiyamma says this, she is exemplifying how closely she identifies her own life with that of her character and how she draws inspiration from it. Leela Panicker has talked about acting in the role of Radha in *Bagnabhavanam*, and continuing to cry for days after, unable to extract herself out of the mental anguish of her character.

These creative and talented actors end up in a world that is entirely male-centric. Direction, choreography, lighting, stage setting, all of it is controlled by men. There are exceptions and they are worth studying. KPAC Sulochana was once asked whether she would ever consider directing a play. 'Well, I haven't tried,' she said. 'When a woman tells them what to do, no one takes her seriously. There have been occasions when Thoppil Bhasi Sir has handed over directing responsibilities to me when he had to go and take care of other matters, busy as he was. But before going away, he would tell the male actors and everyone else—"now Sulochana will be in charge till I'm back." And by the time he came back, I would have moved things forward quite a bit.'

Another example is Iringal Narayani, an actor based in Kozhikode, who has directed plays for several troupes including Yuvashakti Theatres. She has also shown her talent in music direction. Her experiences and contribution to the field of direction, at a time in the 1970s when barely any woman stepped forward in the director's role, have not become part of the history of Malayalam theatre.

'I won't do something I know nothing about,' said a famous actor. 'In any case, no one listens to a woman.' There are many misunderstandings about the art of direction among some women actors, perhaps because directors tend to protect their craft as though it was a secret. 'You can direct a play only if you are fluent in English because many of the words used are in that language,' said an actor who has been active in the field for almost forty years. 'I'm not educated, so I don't have the courage to try.'

Women responding to this topic said that they were quite capable of commenting on the appropriateness of lighting or set design for the plays they are involved in. However, they also believe that in order to be in charge, they need knowledge of specialist language. The issue here is not whether women have the talent to be involved in the production of a play but the atmosphere of secrecy surrounding jobs other than acting.

Citing her own example, Usha Udayan suggests that women theatre workers are quite capable of taking on direction and production. Her husband passed away in a road accident while travelling to a performance. Usha took on the reins of his company, Chaithanya, because she had no other avenue. Her qualification to do this job was the thirteen years she had spent in theatre after having come into the field as an actor in this company. Thus, she began her directorial duties in her own company with the cooperation of her colleagues. 'I was not very confident in the beginning,' she says. 'But I began to envision the stage as a space just like my home where things happened. My acting experience came in handy, as well as the experience of watching my husband direct the plays. I won awards for best director in 1996 and in 2007, and for best female actor in 2000.' Usha believes that women are capable of leading a group and looking after financial matters. 'For a woman actor, directing a play is a big step that is filled with joy and wonderment.'

Ambalappuzha Sreevijaya, who has been active in theatre since 1973, directed the play *Kannukal* for the drama troupe Alappuzha Rajadhani. 'It was well received but didn't make much money, so it ended after fifteen shows,' she says recalling her experience. 'It was when I directed this play that I realized how much knowledge I actually had. Getting to know the characters, lighting, music . . . there are many hard, technical things involved, but there is also satisfaction—the satisfaction of having done something important.'

Meena Ganesh directed the play *Janani* for the railway mahilasamajam (women's group) while she was in the final months of her pregnancy. It brought her an award for best direction.

While the space remained male-dominated, there have been several companies owned and run by women. Women-led antecedents to Usha Vijayan's Chaithanya are Adoor Jaya Theatres started by Adoor Pankajam in 1975, Adoor Matha Theatres led by her sister, Adoor Bhavani in 1980, Kuttyedathi Vilasini's short-run Vishwamatha

Theatres, and Vishwabharathi Theatres owned by Mary Thomas. Kalidasa Kalakendram, one of Kerala's famous drama companies, working for over fifty years, is currently run by Sandhya Rajendran, an alumna of the School of Drama and Fine Arts.

Women's interjections such as these attain significance because of the fact that the theatre is an inherently male domain. The present and continuing impact of these efforts on the language of the theatre are yet to be analyzed.

Womanhood: Real and Imagined

Contemporary professional theatre has a definitive stage language which, of course, is subject to change over time. Theatre audiences are also part of defining this language. There is, in its consolidation, a sort of give and take. Oftentimes, a play is performed not in front of a disciplined, attentive audience, and so, certain gimmicks become part of the production. This impacts character conception as well as acting.

Asked what they thought of the connection between the characters they played and women in real life, most women were of the opinion that 'without relevance and connection to real life, characters cannot live on stage'. There were differing opinions, however. 'There is very little of it in dramas in professional theatre; a bit more realistic in amateur theatre,' said one actor. 'There are a few "good women" characters, essentially those who put up with their husband's oppression,' another person said. 'I get so angry when I have to act in these roles. Even think of changing the dialogue, stuff that you'd never say in real life!'

The plot of a drama is the sum total of a storyline, often based on an incident or life experience that has touched the playwright, as well as the events and action created to tell this story. It will reflect the playwright's worldview and ideological stance. In other words, the playwright interprets or recreates an incident or experience in the context of his worldview and ideology. Reading the history of theatre thus far signals that the fundamental values embodied in these creations are patriarchal.

Discussions about women characters usually found in professional dramas underline the fact that these are more often than not grouped into two—'good women' and 'bad women'. 'Good women' are family-oriented, long-suffering and rarely outspoken, personifying 'the patience of earth itself'. 'Society ladies', feminists, artists, panchayat members, ministers and so on are imagined as diametric opposites to the 'good woman'. Portrayed as different from the norm at the beginning, these 'bad women' often undergo a transformation to become 'good', as a wife or lover. It is not unusual to see women characters, often dressed in modern clothes, characterized as outspoken, ready to challenge anything and not scared to voice her opinion, return to stage in the very next scene demure, dressed in the traditional mundu and veshti, with jasmine in her hair. Masculinity is defined on stage through power, dominance, and violence, while 'adakkam-othukkam'—modesty and control—self-sacrifice and devotedness define femininity.

In these gendered imaginings, especially in creating models of womanhood, the audience is always conceived as masculine. A woman is always defined in comparison with a man. Here, femininity and masculinity are constructed and recreated through a series of stereotypes that emphasize the biological differences between men and women. In professional theatre, directors also define and organize the movement of women characters on stage in such a way that the audience is able to send their clandestine glances beyond the character's presence and into the actor's body. Parallel to this is the situation that a character's importance in the play is directly proportional to the relationship between the actor playing the part and the director. This, many said, is a situation never addressed openly in the field.

Discussions about direction went into styles of direction that demonstrate the power the director wields within theatre. 'Some give good directions; others just sit there saying nothing,' said one person. 'They won't say anything to older actors if they make mistakes. But younger actors like me and newcomers are constantly criticized.' Another said that the woman actor usually is under the full control of the director. 'His presence is made known in every movement, dialogue delivery, which word to stress, everything important and innocuous.' Whether by saying nothing or by interfering in every action, the director ensures that an actor's every movement on stage is defined by him. This points to a situation where the actor internalizes models of womanhood as prescribed by male dominance which defines her identity and indirectly perpetuates existing cultural norms.

Still, even as 'the right way' is always the director's, women have shown the courage and independence to interpret and realize their characters in their own way and make their opinions heard in this regard. The director's demand to 'do as I say' places restrictions on an actor's creativity. And there are ways in which actors work against this restriction. Rather than act in a play as though they were doing a job, many show their individuality through 'refining and polishing' their characters. 'I don't say anything to the director beforehand. I just go on stage and deliver the character in a way that I think is suited to the role,' said one actor, a protest against the existing control over acting.

Every actor makes her own assessment about her acting career, and they have a clear sense of the roles they are able to play and how to play them. 'I read the script several times to get a sense of the kind of acting required,' one person said. 'And I sit in front of the mirror, act the part and make changes and correct mistakes.'

Manakkad Usha is a winner of the Kerala Sangeetha Nataka Akademy award and a veteran of amateur and professional theatre. She was instrumental in bringing S. Sreelatha, a neighbour, into the field. Sreelatha recalls how Usha prepared for her work: 'There was one play in which both Ushachechi and her sister acted. I have a clear memory of the two of them practising, delivering the dialogue and modulating their voices and so on. They took their craft very seriously. Sometimes they would put on the costume and remain in it, even visit neighbours in them. They took such care to understand and deliver each character they played with such dedication.'

Seema G. Nair has similar memories of her mother, Cherthala Sumathi, who was a celebrated artist of her time. 'She was forty-nine when she got the state award for her role as Chiruthakurathi in *Ayiram Suryagayathrikal*. The make-up she had to put on to keep her teeth red for this role gave her chest pain and breathing difficulties. Still, she refused to take it off insisting that the character needed it.'

'My brother and I would sit in front of the mirror, and I would sing and act my part,' remembers KPAC Sulochana. 'It is hard to sing and act at the same time—the strain of singing should not show on the face and cloud the expressions of the character. So I would spend a lot of time preparing before performing on stage.' This dedication, from an actor who was arrested for protesting against the heavy entertainment tax imposed on stage performances, points to her creative and socially conscious identity. Her devotion to her craft is what helped her endure a life strewn with personal losses.

A large majority of actors, contemporary as well as from an earlier era, are not women with professional training even though they have heard of places like the School of Drama and Fine Arts. Acting is a talent they were born with, some said, and that if they were to receive training they would do even better, while others felt that no formal academic study could provide the lessons learned from experience. 'Whatever school you study at or whichever director you work with, there has to be something inherent in the actor. Without it, nothing worthwhile happens.'

Delving into the creative identities of women actors overturns a whole range of assumptions and stereotypes about their existence in society. It points to the fact that, beyond the basic need for employment, their entry into this field is not 'coincidence' or 'accidental' as some of them claim, and that these are in fact social constructs. The position of the woman theatre actor on stage, as well as in society, needs further interrogation. These discussions within the context of Kerala have already moved forward but the community of women actors have not been part of them in any significant manner.

7

Into the World of Contemporary Malayalam Theatre

It was in the 1950s that a concerted attempt began to resist foreign influences in theatre art and find a new language of drama from the roots of Indian performance art. In Kerala, efforts to familiarize and practice this new language were two-pronged: One, the Natakakkalari (theatre workshop) movement focusing on changing the existing culture of theatre and style of performance; and two, Thanathu Natakavedi (indigenous theatre), which sought to bring theatre closer to classical and local art traditions. The language and culture of contemporary Malayalam theatre is a confluence of these two strands.

Natakakkalari: A New Language for Drama

The principle behind Natakakkalari was that formal training was essential not only in writing, performing and acting in drama but also in appreciating it. G. Sankara Pillai, playwright and founder of the movement, makes this clear: 'The objective is to create, in patrons of the dramatic art, an awareness that will help develop a genuine appreciation for it. And to create that awareness, one needs an understanding of how to scientifically analyse a play, examine in detail the medium of the stage, and of the processes that are required to transform a script into a performance through that medium. It is also important to listen to the experiential narratives of those who have worked in the field and managed to keep the flame of their passion alive over time.'[1]

The functioning of Natakakkalari was developed with the inclusion of these considerations. A series of well-attended kalaris took place in Sasthamkotta, Koothattukulam, Dhanuvachapuram and Aluva, followed by others organized by the Kerala Sangeetha Nataka Akademi. For women, this was potentially an opportunity to learn the grammar of a medium that was hitherto kept a secret. But the camps were attended by fewer women than men. Doyens of the theatre, including Gangadharan Pillai and Vayala Vasudevan Pillai, in my conversations with them, remember most women who took part as relatives or acquaintances of the organizers.

In the kalari in Sasthamkotta, Savithrikutty, an English teacher at Thiruvananthapuram Women's College, gave a lecture on the theatre of the absurd. And in Koothattukulam, Annakutty, a teacher from All Saints College, was coerced into acting in the play *Aa Manushyan Nee Thanne*. Savithrikutty was also present at this kalari. Two other teachers from this college had taken part in the kalari on the first day, she said in an interview, but they did not continue because they did not find the male-centric world of the camp comfortable. At the camp in Dhanuvachapuram, the play they worked on was *Samathwavadi*. Lissy Augustine and Vijayam Karunakaran took part in this camp and acted in the play. Vijayam Karunakaran would later move to Delhi and become active in Malayalam theatre there. A few women attended the kalari in Aluva as well where the chosen script was scene 4 of the play *Kanchanaseetha*.

The first Natakakkalari organized by the Sangeetha Nataka Akademi took place between December 1973 and January 1974. A call for applications was published, based on which a preliminary selection of 300 aspirants was made. Sixty-seven of these were invited for interviews, and twenty-five people were selected. Of these, four were women—Baby T. Antony and V. Ramani from Thrissur, and T.T. Sarojini and Molly George from Kozhikode.[2]

The leaders of these camps and the trainers were men. KPAC Sulochana and Mavelikkara Ponnamma were among those invited to share their experiences, but neither was able to attend. The women who did have the opportunity to attend the kalari found it a good experience. Among the women who took part in the second Natakakkalari by the Akademi was Stella, an actor who was active in the 1970s theatre. In my interview with her, she talked about how useful the opportunity was in acquiring a deeper understanding of drama and making the acquaintance of several dignitaries in the field. Bharathi, another actor who had taken part in the Natakakkalari, believes that the lessons she learned there definitely helped form her identity as an actor and in moving her acting life forward. 'Those seven days were a blessing,' she told me. 'I knew nothing about the technical side of drama—lights, setting, even the details involved in acting. Until then, I used to be confused about what to do with my hands when I was on stage, how to place them or use them. At the kalari, Sri Venukkuttan Nair talked to us in detail about such things.'

Not all of the women who took part in these Natakakkalari camps may have had circumstances that allowed them to continue in the field. Nevertheless, for women who came after, the ideas put forth at these camps were useful in asking new questions of the language of drama. The movement also helped in getting highly educated women interested in theatre again.

Beatrice Alex and Savithri Lakshmanan were college teachers when, during the early days of the School of Drama and Fine Arts, they took part in a summer camp on theatre practice organized by their university. This camp, which took place from 2–29 May 1978, was a turning point for both these women as well as for others like Prof. Narendra Prasad, Prof. P. Gangadharan and Prof. Aliyar, who would all become famous in the annals of Malayalam theatre. Beatrice had been active in theatre at the school and college level and had won the Vikraman Nair Trophy for Best Actress in 1966. The camp helped her view stage acting in a new light, she said in her interview with me. No one could skip the well-organized activities; men and women interacted equally in all of them. She remembered that, besides Savithri Lakshmanan, other college teachers were also part of the camp—Parvathi from St Mary's College, Thrissur; Meera from Government College, Pattambi; Rathi Rajan from Providence College, Kozhikode; two nuns from Vimala College, Thrissur; and two women from Tamil Nadu. Beatrice took on the role of Yashoda in G.

Sankara Pillai's play *Snehadoothan* with Prof. Narendra Prasad in the role of the prince, Siddharthan.

When Savithri Lakshmanan participated in the camp, she was beginning to make a name as a playwright. It was her desire to learn more about drama that led her to the camp. She was the mother of an infant at the time, and G. Sankara Pillai allowed her to sit out the physical exercises and also agreed to her request not to act in the play rehearsed at the camp. She participated in the reading of *Oedipus*. The experience, she says, stayed with her and helped drama become an important part also of her teaching life and in her role in bringing several young women into theatre.

N.K. Geetha's participation in Natakakkalari was through a UGC workshop for college teachers in 1982. The forty-two-day camp involved physical exercises, technical aspects, theory as well as practical application in the form of the Malayalam version of Ibsen's play *Ghosts*. Theatre was not alien to Geetha, who came from a family involved in music and dance. Her father, N.K. Vasudeva Panicker, had produced music for several plays, and after having completed her degree, she was managing the dance school her father had started. Perhaps it is this background that saw her participating actively in the physical exercises when many other women were reluctant to take part. Geetha would take forward lessons from this first experience in theatre training and become an important figure in the field of campus theatre.

Natakakkalari helped provide an opportunity for many women to learn about drama and engage deeply with it although those who were able to take this training forward in meaningful ways were predominantly those who already had jobs and an income of their own. These women held on to the lessons learned, took it forward in their work and are still known as good appreciators, organizers and teachers of drama.

Thanathu Natakavedi and Its Trajectories

Efforts to preserve and nurture traditional Indian art forms and, taking inspiration from it, to create a new path for a national theatre, were happening across the country. In Malayalam theatre, it was Kavalam Narayana Panicker who led the way.

In the dramas he wrote, he inculcated a new language unfamiliar to Malayalam theatre until then. This effort was also marked by the significant presence of women theatre workers. In an interview with him, he talked about the women who were part of his efforts in theatre: 'It was quite difficult to find women actors, especially until around 1970. The first woman to collaborate with me was Alissery Ponnamma. Then there was Najarani, the daughter of Klappana Venuji, who played the role of Mannathi in *Daivathar*, and Radhamani, a professional actor, who was part of the verse drama *Sakshi*.'

Kavalam's plays demanded a different set of movements and body language on the stage. They required a keen sense of music and rhythm and perhaps because of this, those who were trained in dance excelled. Examples are Rugmini from Thiruvananthapuram Kalavedi who acted the part of Chithirappennu in *Avanavankadamba*, and the sisters Sujatha and Sunitha in the play *Theyyatheyyam*. A special feature of his plays were roles that demanded the 'natyadharmi' way of performance (stylized or theatre-oriented as opposed to 'lokadharmi', natural or ordinary). He did not believe that men and women required separate or special training; they had to have the same training that helps them draw the flow of energy necessary for realizing the characters mutually. He gave shape to a specialist training based on chari as described in *Natyashastra* (movement of the body below the waist) and Kalari (a form of martial arts in Kerala). Women actors were an active part of this mode of theatre that required intense and long training.

Vasanthakokilam is an actor who came into theatre after her training in Kathakali and Bharathanatyam. She had to face several barriers in order to fulfil her artistic ambitions. She married the actor and theatre aficionado Gopalakrishnan and continued acting on stage. She was a regular in Kavalam's plays and still continues to perform. Other women closely associated with Kavalam's plays are Mohini (*Kallurutti*, *Karimkutty*, *Chilappathikaram*), Sreerekha and Saritha, who is a national Sangeet Natak Akademi awardee. All women who played main characters in Kavalam's plays were trained in dance, denoting the specificity of the female stage language that the plays demanded. Prominent among actors who came to the stage through dance is Leela Panicker, who began her career acting in dramas by Thiruvananthapuram Kalavedi, Sree Chithira Thirunal Granthasala, and Kavalam before associating herself with Natyagraha led by Prof. Narendra Prasad. This range of experience is what makes her life in theatre remarkable. She is one of the people who played a major role in transforming the stage language explored in Natakakkalari and Thanathu Natakavedi movements into a specific language of women on stage.

When the Streets Became Theatre

Theatre camps organized by the Natakakkalari and Thanathu Natakavedi movements and the School of Drama and Fine Arts were the first opportunities women had to gain a deeper understanding of drama and theatre. By the 1980s, there began a women's movement of street theatre, influenced more by the cultural interventions of the 1970s Naxalite movement. This movement changed theatre into a space of onstage debates and the streets into stage. Several plays form part of this movement: *Padayani*, *Amma* (reworking of Gorky's *Mother* and Brecht's *Mother Courage*) and *Spartacus*, all three written by Madhusoodhanan, under the banner of Kozhikode Ranachethana; *Nadugaddika* by K.J. Baby under the banner of Wayanad Samskarikavedi, and *Vellathalamudiyulla Penkutty* from Thrissur. In his book *Ezhupathukal Vilichappol*, playwright and social activist Civic Chandran describes this movement: 'What we tried to do was to provide two functioning legs to drama that was, until then, hobbling along on one leg. The situation then was that where social issues were addressed they ceased to be drama, and when the effort was to make drama a visual medium, it turned into mime.'[3]

The contribution of the Naxalite movement and Samskarikavedi was to once again draw drama closer to the complexities of societal life within which it was formed as well as to give another new dimension to its language. A group of people who had until then only heard of street theatre came together under the leadership of Yakoob, a poet and CPI (ML) activist from Kozhikode, to organize and perform a play on the streets of Kozhikode. For a long time after, in Kerala, street theatre was considered to be the medium of Naxalite groups. In the 1980s, women and Dalit groups began to use street theatre as their medium of choice for communicating their messages.

One of the women actors who actively participated in the plays of the Naxalite movement during this time was Stella, and she had to face many problems because of this. Stella had been part of the second Natakakkalari camp organized by the Sangeetha Nataka Akademi under the leadership of G. Sankara Pillai. After being an active collaborator in the amateur theatre scene, she moved to Wayanad, which is when she began to collaborate in the cultural activities of the Naxalite movement. 'My initial association with them was as an actor,' she recalls, 'and then I had the opportunity to read a lot.' Drawn to Naxalite ideology through her reading, Stella began to act in plays such as *Amma* and *Spartacus*. It was during this time that she met her life partner A.C.K. Raja. Stella remembers this time, which caused great upheaval in her life, fondly and proudly, and believes that the movement and acting gave her the courage to face life's crises.

A play that garnered quite some attention during this period is K.J. Baby's *Nadugaddika*.[4] It was performed by a group including young women from adivasi communities.

'Gaddika' is a custom prevalent among adivasis, especially the Adiyar tribe. This custom, a yearly observance to ward off illness and adversity, was remade onstage as an observance to rid the land of its curses. The play attracted protests at every venue where it was performed, and in the end the entire troupe was arrested and sent to jail. Three adivasi girls who were minors—Makka, Ponni and Leela— were sent to juvenile homes. The women's movement that rose in the 1980s would take great inspiration and momentum from the experiences of these girls and others involved—like Sulochana from Wayanad who spent the entire period of the Emergency in jail for acting in a play— and the new awareness brought about by campus theatre and street theatre.

Women's Experiences of Street Theatre

As with the rest of India, in Kerala too, active women's groups began to form, energized by the first World Conference on Women organized by the United Nations in 1975 and the Declaration of the International Women's Year and the United Nations Decade for Women. Drawing also on the influence of the 1970s street theatre, Manushi, a women's organization based in Pattambi Sreeneelakanda College, performed a street drama in 1986. The play, titled *Sthree* (Woman), was written, directed and performed by women who came out of the campus to make the street its theatre.

'Women teachers and students who were members of Manushi, and their male classmates and colleagues, came out on to the streets with the objective of arousing people's conscience against the increasing atrocities, deaths and suicides relating to the giving and taking of dowry and extravagant weddings,' writes Sarah Joseph, a well-known figure in Malayalam literature. 'Before the play began, students and teachers pledged publicly not to give or take dowry. There was great public support for this play.'[5] In Palakkad, Thrissur, Kozhikode, Wayanad, Kasaragod and Kannur, the play was received enthusiastically by the audience.

> Wake up, rise up, sister
> Wake up, rise up, sister
> Prison of centuries past
> Break up, rise up, sister.

Beginning with these lines, and employing a chorus, the play reflected issues within and outside homes and institutions of law and justice. Several of Kerala's well-known women writers and actors who were teachers and students were involved onstage and offstage in this production, and these included Sarah Joseph, R. Sumangalakutty, N. Parvathi, K.A. Indira, K.M. Rema, Geetha Joseph and K.P. Sreeja. The performance addressed topical events: the rape of fifteen-year-old Latha in Muthalamada in Palakkad; the incident, in Thrissur district, where a young woman named Balamani was paraded naked and ostracized by leaders of her community following a dispute about land boundaries; the 1986 Idukki Thankamani incident of police violence against women in their own homes; and a recent beauty contest. This expression of social activism by a collective of women is in spirit similar to the women of the Antharjana Samajam who wrote and performed *Thozhil Kendrathilekku* in the 1940s.

The 1980s was a time when women's agenda took centre stage in Kerala, and many women's groups and collectives, rooted in feminist ideology, took shape. It ensured that it was difficult for public organizations not to engage with feminist ideas.

During the election period in 1987, another organization, Samatha, was formed in Thrissur. Differing from the independent feminist ideas put forth by Manushi in its plays, Samatha sought to work at the intersection of gender and class. 'It was the deeply felt need to protest against injustice, and the conviction that women should be at the centre of the protests against violence against women, that brought women comrades in and around Thrissur together to form the cultural group Samatha,' recalls T.A. Ushakumari, a teacher at Keralavarma College, Thrissur, who was instrumental in founding the group.[6] She was also the camp director when, towards the end of the 1990s, the Sangeetha Nataka Akademi organized Sthree Nataka Panippura (Women's drama workshop). 'It had students, homemakers, agricultural workers as its members. From 1990 to 1992, Samatha operated out of an office in Laloor, paying a monthly rent of Rs 800. The money made from script and cassette sales as well as donations from the public sustained the organization financially.'[7]

After its formation in 1987, Samatha produced new scripts and songs at the ten-day drama camp in Kolazhi in Thrissur and performed them onstage. This camp was led by N.K. Geetha and Prof. P. Gangadharan. Several young women, interested and invested in leftist ideology, became part of Samatha at various stages—several of them still active in theatre—and these include Vinobha, Sujatha, Pushpa, Anna, Raji, C.S. Chandrika, Kolazhi Bindu, Ramla, Breeze, Sabeena, Sarojini, Sathi, Jolly and Chandramathi. I was one of the people, along with Rosa and Jasmine, who took part in the ten-day camp.

Samatha perfected a style of performance that combined songs, dance choreography and skits, and performed a reworked version of Bertold Brecht's play *Mother Courage*, a choreographed version of his poem 'Concerning the Infanticide, Marie Farrar', *Sathee Matha*, and many others on stage and in street corners. The young women who were part of Samatha underwent great difficulties, including extreme poverty, and what sustained them was their intense social consciousness despite the negligible financial reward they received for their participation. As they worked actively in theatre—singing, dancing and putting up plays—they were subject to bodily threats, disrepute through malicious gossip, and attempts to disrupt their activities.

The 'vanitha kalajadha'—women's art demonstration—organized by the Kerala Sasthra Sahitya Parishad (the people's science and arts movement in Kerala) from 2–22 October 1989, was the continuation of the lively discussions taking place across Kerala about the second-class position of women in social and domestic spheres. The Parishad had begun to look at women's issues with the seriousness that it deserved from 1980. In 1986, after the women's convocation in Valappad, six workshops were organized for the in-depth study of these issues. The discussions that took place on topics such as women and economics, health and energy, law, media, and national and international women's liberation movements gave a sense of direction for the women workers within the Parishad. Women leaders were crucially involved in organizing the two kalajadhas of twenty-two women in 1989. Most of these were Parishad activists or their family members and acquaintances. In less than three weeks, these kalajadhas performed dance choreographies, songs and skits in a 130 places across fourteen districts. Perhaps it was the experience the Parishad had in organizing science and art demonstrations that helped it organize this programme effectively. The slogan of these demonstrations was 'Equality between women and men for the common social good'.

Following this success, in 1990, fifteen more women's kalajadhas were organized on 2,000 stages, with the participation of over 200 women artists. Literacy was the focus of these demonstrations. On 8 March 1993, eight women's kalajadhas—collectively named Samatha—set out to travel across India to raise awareness about women's issues and strengthen the literacy programme, and concluded in Jhansi on 9 April. A large number of young women took active part in the rehearsal camps and performances, leaving their homes, education and work behind temporarily. For many of them, this was a new and exciting experience. The fact that they could relate to the issues being discussed gave them opportunities to rethink and change. However, as artists, their contribution was limited to acting, and was within the parameters of the script and stage language based on ideas and themes already decided without their participation, and written and directed by artists who were part of the Parishad.

The fact is that, in leading such a large group of young women, these organizations held on to several traditional values and norms. One artist remembers that there was a long list of dos and don'ts that they had to follow. 'The jadha made me very happy,' she said. 'We were received enthusiastically wherever we went, and we got to speak to people about women's freedom. But inside the jadha, our freedom was quite heavily controlled.' This need to control women arises from the fact that the good behaviour and discipline that is essential on a long journey is interpreted as the need to discipline and control women.

Despite this, women made these demonstrations lively with their presence on stage, and the experience inspired many of them to choose theatre as their career and equipped them to look more closely at the language of drama in the 1990s. In the visual language of the kalajadhas, the woman who experienced oppression appeared, again and again, in the realistic mode. The conviction that this did not enable the exploration of the complexities involved, or help characterize women as complex beings, began to be prevalent among artists who took the field seriously, leading them to look deeper into the medium that was drama.

8

Of Her Own: The Emergence of Women's Theatre

Understanding women's theatre in Kerala cannot be restricted to the studies about Malayalam theatre history. This theatre—referred to interchangeably as women's theatre and feminist theatre—rose out of feminist engagement and thought. By the end of the 1980s, there were significant women-focused interventions in theories of performance which began to influence theatre history, drama texts and their presentation on stage.

Women's theatre was not about using feminist principles to recognize how a drama text and the structure of its performance define gender and patriarchy. Any text can be given a feminist analysis based on equations of gender and power. The politics of women's theatre went beyond rereading existing texts and performances from a feminist perspective to influencing the construction and structure of theatre itself. It was a new school of thought that would impact the functioning of the theatre and the modes of selection of texts and styles of performances within it. It made crucial contributions to the ever-changing exchange of ideas between art and life. Studies, taking on from feminist scholarship, media studies and politics, put forth several theories and concepts about its definition, role and functioning: as conscious political intervention; as an extension of feminist thought and cultural engagement; as written and performed by women; as theatre that encourages women to dismantle tradition.[1]

The street theatre that emerged out of women's struggles and feminist theatre camps and workshops provided women new ideas and approaches that instigated them to form their own collectives. While mainstream theatre continued to present women in male-defined ways and as individuals without self-identities, women's theatre began to present multi-dimensional women characters who were conscious of their rights, bringing on to the stage their social condition, desires and dreams. Women's worlds envisaged through these productions were not fantasies imagined through the male gaze but a realization of women's aspirations, and the relationships they portrayed—mother, daughter, sister, friend—were all different from those in mainstream drama. Women playwrights set out to imagine and create characters beyond those who orbited around a central male character, and women directors tried to bring in a different mode and style of acting and performance. In order to fulfil these ideological deviations from the mainstream, women's theatre travelled down several diverse paths, consolidating a field that, beyond the presentation of women's experiences, also engaged with the material aspects of gender, class and sexuality. Theatre scholar and director Jeanie Forte has observed that the most difficult aspect for a woman actor is realizing that the characters she performs are not based on the experiences of women.[2]

In the 1990s, feminist theatre in Kerala attempted to make small but decisive and crucial changes to the visual text of the theatre, a task that could be undertaken only by artists well-acquainted with the language of the stage. Learning and teaching this language, watching plays, engaging with dramatic practices in world theatre were all crucial elements in this attempt. Equally important were creating their own spaces to experiment and instigate confidence. Women theatre workers have blazed diverse paths for this task. It is too early to conduct a definitive analysis of these endeavours, so what follows is a description of some of these attempts.

Understanding and Interrogating the Language of Drama

Women who began to make significant interventions in Malayalam theatre in the 1990s included those who had entered the theatre of the 1980s as women's liberation workers, and those who had been part of the Natakakkalari movement and the School of Drama and Fine Arts—in effect, women who had an intimate knowledge of the language of drama. This demands that we see these interventions differently from women's engagement in theatre thus far. These women were interrogating theatre work on a range of levels, finding answers themselves and engaging deeply in creative processes.

Women artists of the 1980s were keenly aware of the fact that, while they participated actively on stage and in street theatre, their role in shaping the language of drama was limited to that of 'acting woman'. Discussions about the fact that societal norms cannot be influenced or changed with the repeated appearance of women on stage as raging rebels, all-suffering family women, and oppressed youth instigated the need to interrogate and analyze drama as a medium.

Equipping Women: Sthree Nataka Camp

It is against this background that a Sthree Nataka Panippura (women's drama camp) was organized in Koothattukulam in December 1992 under the aegis of Sthree Patana Kendram. Sthree Patana Kendram (women's study centre) was a well-known collective of the time, based in Kudamaloor in Kottayam, that ran a women's library and conducted workshops on a variety of topics. Under the leadership of Mini Sukumaran, women from different parts of Kerala regularly took part in its activities. The nataka camp took shape from the conviction that drama was a medium well suited for the public representation of the complexities of women's lives. Street theatre had its limitations, they recognized, and that understanding and using the medium of drama could only be possible if its inherent anti-women ideology was challenged and overcome.

Among those who participated in the camp were social workers, drama students, well-known women artists of the stage as well as women who had little association with the arts world. In 2010, I interviewed S. Sreelatha, who had taken part in the camp. 'What I found most interesting were the improvization classes,' she said. 'So many women who thought in new ways attended and their involvement in these improvization sessions were amazing. There was the limitation of not being familiar with the medium, but the women who were already part of the theatre helped make our participation meaningful.'

The Sthree Patana Kendram in an advertisement leaflet made the thinking and objectives of the workshop clear: 'The drama camp is being organized because of the deeply felt need for strong and successful women's drama troupes. The culture that is currently being presented and promoted in the name of tradition and discipline is leading the society into degeneration and decay. Women are at the receiving end of the violence of this culture that perpetuates dominance and subjugation. It is only through creative exploration that encroachment of these ideas through different media can be challenged and defeated.'

The camp provided a space for women who were interested in getting seriously involved in writing, direction and acting. From 19–25 December 1992, almost sixty women took part in the workshop inaugurated by Chavara Parukkutty, the well-known Kathakali artist. If the camps of the Natakakkalari movement of the 1960s produced a whole line-up of men who took the art of the theatre seriously, this Sthree Nataka camp created many of Kerala's contemporary theatre artists and gave them a new sense of direction. Following on from the workshop, the play *Muditheyyam*, written and directed by K.S. Sreenath and based on Sarah Joseph's short story 'Muditheyyamurayunnu' (Dances the Theyyam of the Locks), was performed for Women's Day celebrations of Thiruvananthapuram Akashvani. I played the main character, Lalitha, in the play, alongside several of Kerala's contemporary theatre artists, including Mini I.G., Rakhi, Mochitha and Alansiyar.

Pioneering a New Language of Drama: Abhinethri

In 1994, three students of drama—C.V. Sudhi, S. Sreelatha (who was already an established actor) and I, Sajitha Madathil—started a drama group called Abhinethri (woman actor). After several days of intense discussions, we decided to produce and perform a drama. The idea was also to be fully involved in the technical side of theatre production. Raghoothaman, who led the drama group 'Abhinaya' in Thiruvananthapuram, allowed us to rehearse in their space. Our first task was to find a suitable text. We decided to create a new text from two of G. Sankara Pillai's plays that we had performed in at various points. These were *Etho Chirakadiyocha* (The Sound of a Flapping Wing) and *Irulilaliyunna Sandhya* (Dusk Melting into Darkness). These plays explored the lives of the mothers of Karna from the Mahabharata: his birth mother, Kunti, and adoptive mother, Radha. *Etho Chirakadiyochakal* shifted the focus of these texts to the mothers who defined themselves around their valiant son and the futility of living such lives. And alongside the main narrative, the play incorporated sarcastic commentary on the lives of women on the Malayalam stage. As women actors who had acted in productions of the original texts led by men directors, our attempt was also to deconstruct the stage language of those performances and create a new one in its place. Part of this was creating and performing an intentional and structured movement that did not limit the female body and overtly challenged the familiar language of performing women on stage. We spent an intense month creating and rehearsing this new feminist language of performance. We were also fully involved in discussions about stage setting, music direction and lighting, led, respectively, by Shaji Karyatt, V. Chandran and Raghoothaman.

The play was performed in Thiruvananthapuram, Thrissur, Ernakulam and Kottayam. In the notice published to announce the first performance, the group made its intentions clear: 'Abhinethri believes that there is space on the stage for women's self-expression, and we intend to explore and experiment with this space. At present, women's involvement in theatre is primarily as actors. We intend to participate in all aspects of theatre, not in tokenistic ways but with the objective of creating a women-specific language of theatre.' Continuing with these intentions, Abhinethri produced the street play *Ente Shareeram Enthethu* (My Body Is Mine) in 1996, and in March 1997 organized a seven-day drama workshop for women.

Around this time, other collectives of women began to form and perform in other parts of the state. These include Medha Theatres in Thiruvananthapuram, headed by C.S. Chandrika, and Dalit Women's Society in Kottayam under the leadership of Rekha Raj. *Urumbukal Samsarikkunnathu*, directed by C.S. Chandrika, and *Vezhcha*, directed by Samkutty, were performed by these groups.

Celebrating Diversity in Women's Theatre: Sangeetha Nataka Akademi Workshop

In 1998, Kerala Sangeetha Nataka Akademi organized a ten-day national workshop on women's theatre in Thrissur. The event included drama training—in which around twenty-five women took part—an exhibition on the history of theatre and classes on various subjects. It also had a festival of drama in which, alongside famous dramatists from outside Kerala, such as Anuradha Kapur, Vibha Mishra, Neelam Mansingh Chowdhry, Mangai, Usha Ganguly and Maya Krishna Rao, Malayali theatre workers—S. Sreelatha, C.S. Chandrika, Divya K., Shylaja S. and I—performed plays.[3]

This festival was a source of great inspiration for women's theatre in Kerala. This opportunity to engage with the productions of a range of women directors from around India firmly rooted the idea in the minds of theatre workers that women's creative expression was not a monolith. It made the audience acknowledge that women's explorations in drama were not superficial experiments but serious engagements with the language of theatre. Through discussions and paper presentations, the workshop also introduced theatre workers to the historical significance of women's theatre and its political and creative manifestations.

Printed on the festival leaflet were the aims and perspectives, which Sarah Joseph laid out for the audience: 1) To explore what constitutes women's theatre; 2) To study in detail feminist drama, and women's body and body language in relation to theatre; 3) To reread history in order to explore how drama became misogynistic; 4) To train women in playwrighting, direction, sound, lighting, stage setting and other technical aspects of theatre.

The event, under the directorship of T.A. Ushakumari, was an acknowledgement of women's intervention in theatre by the Kerala Sangeetha Nataka Akademi. It marked a turning point in how women engaged in amateur theatre with more women coming forward following this. The practice of not paying women other than professional actors was prevalent within amateur theatre until recently. These and other practices began to change with the arrival of women with a background in women's theatre collectives or the School of Drama and Fine Arts into the scene.

Training, Teaching, Growing: The School of Drama and Fine Arts

'When I understood that drama was a subject that required serious study, I decided to join the School of Drama. And was immediately confronted with the first challenging situation—the exercise class in the morning! Men and women taking part in the same exercises. I was reluctant at first, even considered going straight back home. In the initial days, I couldn't move my arms and legs freely, without effort, but soon I began to relax. But throughout it all, I also felt a disquiet, a distress. I yearned to be taught a methodology by someone who understood women's bodies, someone who knew how Kerala's young women's bodies and minds were "tamed". I wouldn't have felt this distressed then.'

This is how S. Sreelatha recalls her days at the School of Drama and Fine Arts. The training there challenged young women, but soon they were able to relax their bodies and open up to the rigours of drama.

The School of Drama and Fine Arts was established in the University of Calicut in 1977, and the first batch in 1978 included women, although fewer in number than men. It marks an important moment in the history of women's involvement in theatre in Kerala. Many of the contemporary actors in the field have a stint at the School of Drama and Fine Arts in their backgrounds.

One of the rising stars in the first batch, Sandhya Rajendran, daughter of O. Madhavan and Vijayakumari, who were both theatre workers, became an accomplished actor and went on to take up the reins of Kalidasa Kalakendram, the professional theatrical group founded by her father. A graduate of the 1985 batch, K.K. Radhamani became a well-known director and directed plays such as *Antigone*, *Chandrodayam*, *Eel*, *Andhar*, etc. She also started the theatre company TOP based in her hometown Peringottukara. Kukku Parameswaran went on to direct C.J. Joseph's play *Crime* for the Thiruvananthapuram-based company Niyogam, before going to London as an actor with Thara Arts Theatre. She is currently a costume designer in Malayalam cinema and, in collaboration with S. Sreelatha, conducts drama workshops for college students.

Several such stories exist that underline how a rigorous and structured immersion in drama can open up avenues for talented young women. However, there are also equally compelling stories that point to the need for embedding gender sensitive and women-centric policies and practices within the institution.

'When I joined the school, I was already acting in a production of Vayala Sir's *Kuchelavritham*,' recalls Jisha who had to leave halfway through her course. 'I had to fulfil this commitment, but when I went to do the next two performances, senior students at the school created a furore saying that it was against the rules. I was three months pregnant then and couldn't take all the aggravation and had to make the decision to leave the course I had joined with so much hope and desire.'

When Kani Kusruti, who acted as Nurse Prabha in the film *All We Imagine as Light*, which won the Grand Prix at the 2024 Cannes Film Festival, joined the School of Drama and Fine Arts, she was already an experienced actor having been involved with the Thiruvananthapuram-based Abhinaya from a young age. Her stint at the school too was short-lived: she left early, disturbed by the male-centric atmosphere and dissatisfied with the learning environment. Kani went on to study at L'École Internationale de Théâtre Jacques Lecoq in Paris.

For many women who have undergone rigorous study and training, theatre still does not provide a primary source of livelihood. They continue in the field while also dealing with the difficulties of holding down a full-time job and taking care of their families. That they find the energy and enthusiasm to continue as stage actors is a testament to the fact that they see the stage as the space for their creative expression. Among them are renowned contemporary actors such as Sailaja M.G. (a bank employee), Geetha Joseph (principal of a higher secondary school), Beena (a teacher), Jisha (a journalist), Anithakumari (a medical representative), Sukanya Shaji (an advocate) and several others.

The Varied Paths of Women's Theatre

Women's insistent presence, sometimes against all odds, has brought about many changes in drama troupes and companies. Going beyond their expected roles as women who 'came, acted and went away', and armed with the experience of studying drama as a discipline and engaging in women's theatre initiatives, their presence engendered discomfort in these male-defined creative collectives. However, it is possible to see that some theatre companies are slowly beginning to embrace this changed role of women—from actors to theatre workers. Plays directed by men began, at least in a limited sense, to embrace women-centric themes and ideologies. In the process, a politics of feminist theatre developed and organically became an important strand in the world of Malayalam theatre. The paths forged by some of these groups, playwrights, actors, directors, and other theater workers are explored below.

In 1999, the women's drama group Nireeksha was established in Thiruvananthapuram. Alongside producing and performing feminist dramas, Nireeksha aimed to conduct workshops for women and children and organize drama festivals and seminars. Actively working behind the scenes at Nireeksha were the playwright E. Rajarajeswari and director C.V. Sudhi. Nireeksha's productions include *Kudiyozhikkal*, *Pravachaka*, *Anungalillatha Pennungal*,

Punarjani, *Avathar*, *Varthamanakam* and *Kanalthuruthu*. The artists at Nireeksha were fully aware that a women's drama troupe putting down deep roots in Kerala is an arduous task. And they were convinced that developing a women-oriented methodology for collectivism and collaboration, and a style of direction that centres women, were as important as performing feminist dramas. Overcoming several barriers over the years, Nireeksha is now well-established in the theatre world, with a salary grant from the central government and a grant for light equipment. Nireeksha is also one of the few women's theatre groups that has its own theatre space.

In Thrissur district, theatre worker Sreeja Arangottukara is involved in community work along with her family. Women's collectives have been central in her work in the theatre. 'I became close to the theatre world through Manushi, the women's collective,' Sreeja recollects. 'Feminists, including Sarah Joseph, who spoke at campus theatres taught us that drama can be used as an effective political weapon.' Sreeja says that she has not experienced much of the discomfort that comes with a community's response to performing in rural areas. 'Sneers such as "acting woman" and "loose" have not been used against me, perhaps because I was more often described as "Naxalite" and "feminist". Or perhaps because I became active in theatre while living with Narayanan who thinks theatre is his whole life!'

Drawing energy from her collective and community work, Sreeja centres feminist thought in the dramas she writes and directs. In *Ororo Kalathilum* (At Each Time), travelling from the present to the past and back, she explored how a woman's love was often singed in the fire of a man's lust, and how in the final analysis, time is only an indication of distance.[4] The main character in the play, Thathri, is based on the historical figure Kuriyedath Thathri, a Namboothiri woman who was subjected to 'smarthavicharam'— 'inquiry into the conduct', which was a community trial of women accused of immoral conduct which led to their ostracization from home and community—in 1905. Thathri and young women subjected to sexual violence like in the Suryanelli rape case were victims separated by the distance of time. However, unlike Thathri who had the signet ring of her attacker to produce as evidence, women of a new age had nothing to support them when they spoke up. The play echoed, as though in advice to the women of the present, Thathri's unforgettable words, 'look for your path with your own eyes,' reminding the audience of the inherent helplessness in the lives of women in Kerala as well as the necessity of forging our own solutions. Her other plays, *Kalakariyude Katha*, *Parethathmavinte Saropadesham*, *Kattukondu Veeduvekkunnavar* and *Idanilangal* co-written with Dineshan are all being performed regularly on stages across Kerala. Sreeja is also a founding member of Kala Patasala, an organization that foregrounds environmental issues and women's politics.

Shylaja M.G. was the first Malayali woman to attain a degree, in 1998, in direction and design from the National School of Drama (NSD) in New Delhi. She received a study grant from Asian Art Network and participated in the Asian Theatre Festival in 2000 in Tokyo. She has directed six plays including *Thathri: Realising Self*, a play in Hindi produced with a grant from Majlis in Mumbai. This play is also based on the story of Kuriyedath Thathri, retold from a contemporary point of view.

Another alumna of NSD is Mini I.G., who graduated in the year 2000. Active in the theatre scene in Balussery in Kozhikode since 1995, Mini set up the group Host-O-Theatre in 2000 and began to engage more widely in Malayalam theatre. She has directed six plays including the Hindi drama, *Andora*, and in all her plays, Mini also takes on responsibilities for costume and set design. Mini directed the play *Meira Paibi* by Civic Chandran, which was performed in various venues across India as part of the national campaign in support of Irom Sharmila, the civil rights activist from Manipur. A Charles Wallace fellow, Mini has held exhibitions of the posters she designed for her plays, and is currently actively involved in cinema as director, scriptwriter and actor.

As a young woman, I too left Kerala in the early 1990s to study drama, first to Rabindra Bharati University in Kolkata for a master's degree in stage acting and then, with a fellowship from the Japanese Foundation, to Jawaharlal Nehru University to do a PhD. I received my doctorate in the history and contributions of women in Malayalam theatre. I performed in plays in Kolkata and Delhi, and worked with a drama troupe in South Africa. The plays I have written include *Matsyagandhi* (mono-play), *Chakkeechankaran: A Family Reality Show*, *Mother's Day*, *Kali Natakam* and *She Archive*.[5] I performed *Matsyaganghi* and another mono-play, *Beauty Parlour* (co-written and co-directed with K.S. Sreenath), on several stages in and outside Kerala.

S. Sreelatha, a regular presence in the 1970s amateur theatre in Thiruvananthapuram, went to study at the School of Drama and Fine Arts, encouraged by playwrights Venukuttan Nair and G. Sankara Pillai. As we have already seen, she had a key role in setting up Abhinethri. After taking part in the workshops they conducted in Thiruvananthapuram, the French touring theatre company, Footsbarn Theatre, accepted her as a member, and she went on a world tour with them until 2007. She directed K.S. Sreenath's *Devasilakal* and the mono-play *Savithrikutty*, for which she also prepared the script.

The experiences of these women show that they have made every effort to understand and apply the grammar of a medium they were not familiar with, in the process pushing against barriers and boundaries and using every opportunity available to them. They manage their difficult work situations, juggling rehearsals, leading groups, dealing with finances and their daily responsibilities outside theatre. In my interviews with them, several of these women said that although at times embracing drama as their way of life can feel like an ember smouldering slowly, they could not think of giving up walking down these creative paths.

Playing Solo

Contemporary Malayalam theatre is marked by a considerable number of women who perform freelance and in mono-plays. The choice to do so arose from the isolating nature of theatre, as well as the discomfort that still exists within it. For many women mono-players—such as Jisha who has performed several of them, Rajitha Madhu who performed Karivalloor Murali's *Abubakerude Umma Parayunnu*, Madonna and Thani who both performed Civic Chandran's *Meira Paibi*, Elsy Sukumaran who delivered *Hidumbi* directed by Jayaprakash Karyat, Rathi Eravathur who performed *Ekakini* directed by A. Santhakumar, Shiny Pookkad who performed *Amen*—choosing this medium was a way of finding the most appropriate mode to express their creativity that would best accommodate their life circumstances. For women's theatre, mono-play was an important language of drama, one that became significant in the absence of enabling theatre collectives or circumstances that allowed participating in collective work.

Creating Inspiring Environments

Women artists brought about significant, decisive changes in writing plays as well as performing them, thereby clearing a path for many other women to enter the theatre. Their work, in the spirit of give and take and exchanging ideas and skills, continues to strengthen the field. Women's theatre work collaborates with feminist groups to advance women's concerns and creativity. An example is the performance of Snehalatha Reddy's play *Sita*, collaboratively produced by the women's theatre group Nireeksha and the feminist collective Anveshi based in Kozhikode. By centring feminist thought, these productions attempt to break away from traditional ideas about women's body language and representation in the public sphere of the theatre.

Since 1997, the Kerala government has instituted a programme named Kudumbashree, which aims to empower women and ensure financial independence in the community.[6] Drama groups named Rangashree, organized by Kudumbashree workers have become a part of its activities in all districts in Kerala. Nireeksha's workshops have been instrumental in identifying artists among this group of women, and Kerala Sangeetha Nataka Akademi organized drama workshops for them as part of its International Theatre Festival of Kerala (ITFOK). These workshops were opportunities for ordinary, talented women to learn from and interact with renowned theatre workers from India and abroad. Rangashree's activities are another milestone in the political involvement of women in theatre.

Engaging creatively in the male-dominated public space of Kerala is a difficult task for the woman artist. A large number of them do this work while fully accepting or strategically managing the responsibilities placed on them by the institution of the family, and while working for its financial survival. The most important contribution of women's theatre is that it has helped in creating an environment that inspires, supports and sustains them.

The significance of this specific stream of work within Malayalam theatre is that it has succeeded in liberating women artists from their limiting role of 'acting woman' and set them free as theatre workers who are capable of engaging fully in its creative, aesthetic and technical language and realization. And in fulfilling this task, they honour their ancestors—the women who history forgot; the women who, despite all difficulties, left their indelible presence in theatre, from sangeetha natakam to reformation theatre, to social and political dramas. The women who loved their art and persevered against all odds.

References

Books and Articles

Abraham, Vinu. *Nashta Nayika*. Thrissur: Current Books, 2008.

Anandi, T.K. *Janakeeya Samarangalil Malabarinte Penpathakal—Devaki Narikkattiri*. Thrissur: Kerala Sasthra Sahitya Parishad, 2006.

Antharjana Samajam. *Thozhil Kendrathilekku*. Thrissur: Yogakshema Press, 1948.

Antharjanam, Lalithambika. *Lalithambikayude Randu Natakangal*. Kottayam: National Book Stall, 2014.

Antharjanam, Lalithambika. *Athmakathakku Oru Aamukham*. Thrissur: Current Books, 1979.

Antony, P.J. *P.J. Antoniyude Sampoorna Krithikal*, Vol. 1. Kottayam: Sahitya Pravarthaka Sahakarana Sangham, 2015.

Aston, Elaine. *Feminist Theatre Practice: A Handbook*. London: Routledge, 1999.

Ayamu, E.K. *Jju Nalloru Mansanakan Nokku*. Thiruvananthapuram: Chintha Publishers, 2011.

Ayisha, Nilambur. *Jeevithathinte Arangu*. Thiruvananthapuram: Women's Collective, 2005.

Baby, K.J. *Nadugaddika*. Thrissur: Current Books, 1983.

Bhagavathar, Sebastian Kunjukunju. *Natakasmaranakal*. Thrissur: Kerala Sangeetha Nataka Akademi, 1986.

Bhasi, Madavoor. *Malayala Nataka Sarvaswam*. Thiruvananthapuram: Chaitanya Publications, 1990.

Bhasi, Thoppil. *Ningalenne Communistakki*. (1956). Kottayam: DC Books, 1988.

Bhaskaranunni, P. *Pathompatham Noottandile Keralam*. Thrissur: Kerala Sahitya Akademi, 1988.

Bhattathiripad, M.P. *Rithumathi*. Thiruvananthapuram: Maluben Publications, 2018.

Bhattathiripad, M.R. *Marakkudakkullile Mahanarakam*. Thrissur: G. Sankara Pillai Smaraka Nataka Patana Kendram, 1997.

Bhattathiripad, V.T. *Adukkalayilninnu Arangathekku*. Kottayam: DC Books, 1999.

Bhattathiripad, V.T. *VTyude Sampoorna Krithikal*. Kottayam: DC Books, 1997.

Binu, K.D. and Manosh Manoharan. 'Absence in Presence: Dalit Women's Agency, Channar Lahala, and Kerala Renaissance.' *Journal of International Studies*, Vol. 22, Issue 10, Article 3, 2021.

Canning, Charlotte. 'Theorizing a Feminist Theatre History.' *Theatre Journal*, Vol. 45, No. 4, 1993.

Chandran, Civic. *Ezhupathukal Vilichappol*. Mavelikkara: Fabian Books, 2009.

Chandumenon, O. *Indulekha*. (Self-published 1889). Translated by Anitha Devasia. Hyderabad: Oxford University Press, 2005.

Cherukad. *Jeevithapatha*. Thrissur: Chintha Publishers, 1994.

Cherukad. *Nammalonnu*. Thiruvananthapuram: Chintha Publishers, 1988.

Cherukad. *Nammalonnu* (Revised version). Thrissur: Current Books, 1988.

Damodaran, K. *Pattabakki*. Kottayam: National Book Stall, 1956.

Devika, J. *Nirantharaprathipaksham*. Kottayam: DC Books, 2021.

Devika, J., ed. *Kalpanayude Mattoli: Gender and Early Writings of Malayalee Women, 1898–1938*. Thrissur: Kerala Sasthra Sahitya Parishad, 2011.

Edasseri, Govindan Nair. *Koottukrishi*. Kozhikode: Poorna Publications, 2002.

Forte, Jeanie. 'Women's Performance Art: Feminism and Postmodernism.' In *Performing Feminisms: Feminist Critical Theory and Theatre*, edited by Sue-Ellen Case. Baltimore: Johns Hopkins University, 1990.

Geenakumari, T. *P.K. Medini. Viplavavazhiyile Vanambadi*. Thrissur: Samatha Publications, 2019.

Geetha. *Penkalangal*. Thrissur: Current Books, 2010.

Gopalakrishnan, Chelangatt. *Annathe Nayikamar*. Kottayam: DC Books, 2012.

Gopalakrishnan, P.K. *Purogamana Sahitya Prasthanam: Nizhalum Velichavum*. Thrissur: Kerala Sahitya Akademi, 1987.

Ikkavamma, Thottakkattu. *Subhadrarjunam*. Thrissur: Prof. P. Sankaran Nambiar Foundation, 2002.

Jose, C.L. *Natakathinte Kanapurangal*. Kottayam: DC Books, 1996.

Joseph, Sarah. *Bhoomirakshasam*. Kannur: Kairali Books, 2009.

Kelappan, K. 'Preface.' In *Adukkalayilninnu Arangathekku* by V. T. Bhattathiripad. Kottayam: DC Books, 1999.

Kerala Sangeetha Nataka Akademi. *Nadodi Drishyakala Soochika*. Thrissur: Kerala Sangeetha Nataka Akademi, 1978.

Kesavan, C. *Jeevithasamaram*. Kottayam: DC Books, 2004.

Krishnapilla, Thoppil. *Ezhayiram Ravukal—Memoir*. Thrissur: Current Books, 1996.

Kumar, Hemanth. *Lakshmi, Adhava Arangile Anarkali*. Unpublished manuscript. 2017.

Kumar, Udaya. 'Ambivalence of Publicity: Transparency and Exposure in K. Ramakrishna Pillai's Writings.' In *The Public Sphere from Outside the West*, edited by V. Sanil and Divya Dwivedi. London: Bloomsbury, 2015.

Lerner, Gerda. *The Majority Finds its Past*. New York: Oxford University Press, 1979.

Madathil, Sajitha. *Arangile Matsyagandhikal*. Thrissur: Green Books, 2018.

Madathil, Sajitha. *Aranginte Vakabhedangal*. Kottayam: DC Books, 2013.

Madathil, Sajitha. *M.K. Kamalam*. Thiruvananthapuram: Kerala State Chalachitra Academy, 2010.

Mani, Kunnukuzhi. *P.K. Rosy: Malayala Cinemayude Amma*. Thiruvananthapuram: Maithri Books, 2019.

Mani, Kunnukuzhi. *J.C. Daniel*. Thiruvananthapuram: Maithri Books, 2017.

Mannummood, C.J. 'Samoohya Parishkaranonmukhamaya Adyathe Swathanthra Natakam,' Preface. In *Mariyamma Natakam* (7th edition) by Palachirackal Kocheeppan Tharakan. Kottayam: Sahitya Pravarthaka Sahakarana Sangham, 2001.

Mohandas, Vallikkadu. *KPACyude Charithram*: Kayamkulam: People's Arts Club, 2002.

Nair, Bhaskaran V., ed. *Kutti Kunju Thankachiyude Krithikal*. Thrissur: Kerala Sahitya Akademi, 1979.

Nair, Muralidharan V. *Natakam Jeevithamakkiyavar*. Kottayam: DC Books, 1981.

Namboothiripad, EMS. *Communistaya Natakakrithu: Thoppil Bhasi Smaranika*. Unknown publisher, 2001.

Narayanan, Kattumadam. *Malayala Natakathiloode*. Palakkad: Udaya Publications, 1960.

Padmanabhan, K.P. *Kochi Rajya Charithram*. Thrissur: Mathrubhumi Books, 2021.

Panicker, K.N. 'Indulekha: Oru Punarvayana.' *Samvadam*, Issue 1, May–June, 1989.

Pillai, G. Sankara. *Naandi: Natakakkalariyile Prabhashanangalum Swanubhavangalum, 1973–74*. Kottayam: National Book Stall, 1974.

Pillai, G. Sankara, *Malayala Nataka Sahitya Charithram*. Thrissur: Kerala Sahitya Akademi, 2005.

Pillai, Vayala Vasudeva. 'Study.' In *Marakkudakkullile Mahanarakam* by M.R. Bhattathiripad. Thrissur: G. Sankara Pillai Smaraka Nataka Patana Kendram, 1997.

Raghavan, Puthuppally, ed. *C. V. Kunhiramante Thiranjedutha Krithikal*. Thiruvananthapuram: Kaumudi Public Relations Department, 1974.

Rajalakshmi, B.R. 'Punarjanmam Thedi Oru Savithrikutty.' *Granthalokam*, March, 1997.

Sai, Veejay. *Drama Queens: Women Who Created History on Stage*. New Delhi: Roli Books, 2017.

Sreeja, K. V. *Ororo Kalathilum*. Kottayam: DC Books, 2004.

Sreekumar, K. *Ochira Velukutty: Jeevacharithram*. Thrissur: Kerala Sahitya Akademi, 2006.

Sreekumar, K. *Our Mukham: Janapriya Natakavediyude Midippukal*. Kozhikode: Lipi Publications, 2005.

Sreekumar, K. *Malayala Sangeetha Nataka Charithram*. Thrissur: Current Books, 2002.

Sreekumar, Kureepuzha. 'Natiyude Rathri.' in *The Heroine*, edited by Sunil C.E. Thiruvananthapuram: Saketham Publications, 2018.

Srinivasan, Janaki. 'Paradox of Human Development of Women in Kerala.' *Economic and Political Weekly*, Vol. 44, No. 10, 2009.

Sulochana, KPAC. *Arangile Anubhavangal*. Thrissur: Current Books, 2007.

Thomas, C.J. *Uyarunna Yavanika*. Kottayam: National Book Stall, 2010.

Ulloor, S. Parameswara Iyer. *Kerala Sahitya Charithram, Vol. 4*. Thrissur: Kerala University Publication Department. 1974.

Unniraja, C. 'Preface.' In *Ningalenne Communistakki*. (1956) by Thoppil Bhasi. Kottayam: DC Books, 1988.

Ushakumari, T.A., ed. *Thozhil Kendrathilekku: Natakam, Charithrarekha, Patanam*. Thrissur: Samatha Publications, 2014.

Venkitaraman, C.S. and Arathy Ashok. *The Lost Heroine*. New Delhi: Speaking Tiger, 2020.

Vijayakumari. 'Chitta Nalkiya Kalari.' *Bhashaposhini*, November, 1998.

Weblinks and Miscellany

Ashraf, Mohammed. 'E.K. Ayamu, Jju Nalloru Mansanakan Nokku.' https://www.mlylm.in/2017/03/ek-ayamu-nilambur.html

Edasseri, Govindan Nair. 'Kavitha Ente Jeevithathil.' Vishalakeralam. https://www.edasseri.org/Essays-EdasseriLiterature/KavithaEnteJeevithathil-Edasseri.pdf

Nair, Gopinathan T.N. 'Marthandavarma Muthal Samasamam Vare.' Sree Chithira Thirunal Granthasala Golden Jubilee Souvenir, 1966.

Sebastian, Meryl Mary. 'The Name of the Rose.' The Big Indian Picture, June 2013. https://thebigindianpicture.com/2013/06/the-name-of-the-rose/

Ushakumari, T.A. 'Keralathile Sthreekal.' Paper presented at the seminar, 'Samatha: Utbhavavum Valarchayum.' February 11–12, Thiruvananthapuram, 1995.

Notes

Author's Note

1 Pillai, G. Sankara. *Malayala Nataka Sahitya Charithram*. Thrissur: Kerala Sahitya Akademi, 2005. p. 13.

Chapter 1: Out of the Shadows, Gently: Women and the Birth of Theatre in Kerala

1 The state of Kerala was founded on November 1, 1956. In the nineteenth century, the Malayalam-speaking region that is currently Kerala was made up of Thiruvithamkoor, Kochi and Malabar. However, for ease of reference, I have used 'Kerala' throughout this book, except when speaking about a specific region within its current boundary.

2 Binu, K.D. and Manosh Manoharan. 'Absence in Presence: Dalit Women's Agency, Channar Lahala, and Kerala Renaissance.' *Journal of International Women's Studies*, Vol. 22, Issue 10, Article 3, 2021.

3 Padmanabhamenon, K.P. *Kochi Rajya Charithram*. (New edition). Thiruvananthapuram: Mathrubhumi Books, 2021.

4 Bhaskaranunni, P. *Pathombatham Noottandile Keralam*. Thrissur: Kerala Sahitya Akademi, 1988. p. 751.
5 Kesavan, C. *Jeevithasamaram*. Kottayam: DC Books, 2004. p. 67.
6 Ibid., p. 70.
7 Ibid., p. 73.
8 Raghavan, Puthuppally, ed. *C.V. Kunhiramante Thiranjedutha Krithikal*. Thiruvananthapuram: Kaumudi Public Relations, 2002. p. 220.
9 Nair, Bhaskaran V., ed. *Kutti Kunju Thankachiyude Krithikal*. Thrissur: Kerala Sahitya Akademi, 1979.
10 Ulloor, S. Parameswara Iyer. *Kerala Sahitya Charithram Vol. 4*. Thiruvananthapuram: Kerala University Publication Department, 1974. p. 273.
11 Ikkavamma, Thottakkattu. *Subhadrarjunam* (First edition 1891). Thrissur: Prof P. Sankaran Nambiar Foundation, 2002.
12 Ulloor, *Kerala Sahitya Charithram*, p. 274.
13 Referred to widely as 'the father of modern Malayalam literature'. Thunchath Ezhuthachan was the author of *Adyathmaramayanam Kilippattu*, the Malayalam version of The Ramayana. Kilippattu (birdsong) is a genre of Malayalam poetry where the narrator is a parrot or a swan or a bee and so on.
14 Ikkavamma, *Subhadrarjunam*. p. 18.
15 Ulloor, *Kerala Sahitya Charithram*, p. 497. There are a few references in documents from the time that 'Ikkavamma of Ramanchira Matam' and Thottakkattu Ikkavamma were the same person. However, some doubt still remains.
16 Bhasi, Madavoor. *Malayala Nataka Sarvaswam*. Thiruvananthapuram: Chaithanya Publications, 1990.

Chapter 2: Rivalling Real Women: Female Impersonation in Tamil and Malayalam Musical Dramas

1. Sai, Veejay. *Drama Queens: Women Who Created History on Stage*. New Delhi: Roli Books, 2017.
2. Kumar, Udaya. 'Ambivalences of Publicity: Transparency and Exposure in K. Ramakrishna Pillai's Writings'. In *The Public Sphere from Outside the West*, edited by V. Sanil and Divya Dwivedi. London: Bloomsbury, 2015, pp. 79–96.
3. Sreekumar, K. *Malayala Sangeetha Nataka Charithram*. Thrissur: Current Books, 2002.
4. Sreekumar, K. *Ochira Velukkutty: Jeevacharithram*. Thrissur: Kerala Sangeetha Nataka Akademi, 2006.
5. Ibid., p. 99.
6. Ibid., p. 100.
7. Ibid.
8. Bhagavathar, Sebastian Kunjukunju. *Natakasmaranakal*. Thrissur: Kerala Sangeetha Nataka Akademi, 1986. p. 184.
9. Ibid., p. 50.
10. Ibid., p. 370.
11. Nair, Muralidharan V. *Natakam Jeevithamakkiyavar*. Kottayam: DC Books, 1981. p. 69.

Chapter 3: Into the Limelight: Early Heroines of Musical and Social Theatre

1. Bhagavathar, Sebastian Kunjukunju. *Natakasmaranakal*. Thrissur: Kerala Sangeetha Nataka Akademi, 1986. pp. 227–230.
2. Devika, J. ed. *Kalpanayude Mattoli: Gender and Early Writings of Malayalee Women, 1898–1938*. Thrissur: Kerala Sasthra Sahithya Parishath, 2011, p. 16.

3. Amma, L. Meenakshikutty. 'Women's Unemployment'. In *Kalpanayude Mattoli*, pp. 47–54.
4. Srinivasan, Janaki. 'Paradox of Human Development of Women in Kerala.' *Economic and Political Weekly*, Vol. 44, No. 10, pp. 23–25, p. 2009.
5. Devika, J. *Nirantharaprathipaksham*. Kottayam: DC Books, 2021. pp. 35–45.
6. Bhagavathar, *Natakasmaranakal*. p. 57.
7. Sebastian, Meryl Mary. 'The Name of the Rose'. June 2013. http://thebigindianpicture.com/2013/06/the-name-of-the-rose/ [Retrieved 06 June 2024].
8. Abraham, Vinu. *Nashta Nayika*. Thrissur: Current Books, 2008. p. 17. An English translation by C.S. Venkiteswaran and Arathy Ashok, titled *The Lost Heroine*, was published in 2020 by Speaking Tiger.
9. Kerala Sangeetha Nataka Akademi. *Natoti Drishyakala Soochika*. Thrissur: KSNA. 1978. p. 48.
10. Sebastian, 'The Name of the Rose'.
11. Abraham, *Nashta Nayika*, p. 18.
12. Sebastian, 'The Name of the Rose'.
13. Ibid.
14. Mani, Kunnukuzhi. *P.K. Rosy: Malayala Cinemayude Amma*. Thiruvananthapuram: Maithri Books, 2019.
15. Mani, Kunnukuzhi. *J.C. Daniel*. Thiruvananthapuram: Maithri Books, 2017.
16. Ibid., pp. 11–13.
17. Ibid.
18. Ibid.
19. Sreekumar, Kureepuzha. 'Natiyude Raathri.' In *The Heroine*, edited by Sunil C.E. Thiruvananthapuram: Saketham Publications, 2018. pp. 9–11.

20 Gopalakrishnan, Chelangatt. *Annathe Nayikamar*. Kottayam: DC Books, 2012.
21 Mani, *P.K. Rosy: Malayala Cinemayude Amma*, p. 45.
22 Ibid., p. 47.
23 Sebastian, 'The Name of the Rose'.
24 Ibid.
25 *Lakshmi, Adhava Arangile Anarkali*. Hemanth Kumar (writer), Manoj Narayanan (director), Kozhikode Sankeerthana (production). Unpublished text.
26 Bhagavathar, *Natakasmaranakal*, p. 232.
27 Ibid., p. 231.
28 Sreekumar, K. *Oru Mukham: Janapriya Natakavediyude Midippukal*. Kozhikode: Lipi Publications, 2005. p. 90.
29 Bhagavathar, *Natakasmaranakal*, p. 255.
30 Ibid.
31 Ibid., pp. 373–374.
32 Sreekumar, *Oru Mukham*, p. 93.
33 Bhagavathar, *Natakasmaranakal*, p. 373.
34 Bhasi, Madavoor. *Malayala Nataka Sarvaswam*. Thiruvananthapuram: Chaithanya Publicatons, 1990, p. 421. Varkala Ammukutty is mentioned in a few places in Sebastian Kunjukunju Bhagavathar's memoirs, *Natakasmaranakal* (1986). He says he had heard that the first woman to step up to the stage was Varkala Ammukkutty, even though he had never met her. Written documents and photographs about her performing in the play *Vyazhavattathinushesham* are preserved at the Sree Chithira Thirunal Library, Thiruvananthapuram.
35 Gopalakrishnan, Chelangatt. *Annathe Nayikamar*. Kottayam: DC Books, 2012. p. 95.

36 Ibid.
37 Ibid., p. 94.
38 Bhagavathar, *Natakasmaranakal*, p. 294.
39 Until the end of the third decade of the twentieth century, like most temples in Kerala, the Shiva temple in Vaikom in Thiruvithamkoor refused entry to people from the lower castes. They were also banned from using the roads near the temple. Spearheaded by T.K. Madhavan, K. Kelappan and others, Vaikom Satyagraham was a non-violent protest against this practice that took place between March 1924 and November 1925. This was one of the agitations that led to the Temple Entry Proclamation in Thiruvithamkoor in 1936.
40 Ibid., p. 375.
41 Madathil, Sajitha. *M.K. Kamalam*. Thiruvananthapuram: Kerala State Chalachithra Academy, 2010. pp. 24–25.
42 Ibid., pp. 25–26.
43 Ibid., pp. 40.
44 Gopalakrishnan, *Annathe Nayikamar*. p. 47.
45 Madathil, *M.K. Kamalam*, pp. 61–62.
46 Ibid., pp. 62–63.
47 Sreekumar, *Oru Mukham*, p. 103.

Chapter 4: Making a New Malayali Woman: Women's Agenda in the Theatre

1 Mannummood, C.J. 'Samoohya Parishkaranonmukhamaya Adyathe Swathanthra Natakam.' Preface. In *Mariyamma Natakam*. 7th Edition. Polachirackal Kocheeppan Tharakan. Kottayam: Sahithya Pravarthaka Sahakarana Sangham, 2001.

2 Nair, T.N. Gopinathan. *Marthandavarma Muthal Samamsamam Vare*. Sree Chithira Thirunal Granthasala Golden Jubilee Souvenir, 1966. p. 16.
3 Bhasi, Madavoor. *Malayala Nataka Sarvaswam*. Thiruvananthapuram: Chaithanya Publications, 1990. p. 13.
4 Nair, T.N. Gopinathan. *Marthandavarma Muthal Samamsamam Vare*.
5 I have not been able to find more information about the all-women troupe founded by Thankam, not even its name. We do, however, know that Ikkavamma's *Subhadrarjunam* was performed several times by her daughter, Thottakkattu Madhavi Amma.
6 Excerpt from Mini Sukumar's interview with Saraswathi Amma as part of Sthree Nataka Panippura (women's drama camp), Thiruvananthapuram.
7 Kelappan, K. 'Preface'. In *Adukkalayilninnu Arangathekku*. V.T. Bhattathiripad. Kottayam: DC Books, 1999. p. 13.
8 Chandumenon, O. *Indulekha*. Self-published 1889. Multiple translations into English exist, the most recent by Anitha Devasia, published by Oxford University Press, Hyderabad, in 2005.
9 Panicker, K.N. 'Indulekha Oru Punarvayana.' *Samvadam*, Issue 1, May–June, 1999. p. 13.
10 Bhattathiripad, V.T. *Adukkalayilninnu Arangathekku*. Kottayam: DC Books, 1999, p. 69.
11 Bhattathiripad, M.R. *Marakkudakkullile Mahanarakam*. Thrissur: G. Sankarapillah Smaraka Nataka Patana Kendram, 1997.

12 Pillai, Vayala Vasudevan. 'Marakkudakkullile Prakashadhara—Study'. In *Marakkudakkullile Mahanarakam*. p. 17.
13 Anandi, T.K. *Janakeeya Samarangalil Malabarinte Penpathakal—Devaki Narikkattiri*. Thrissur: Kerala Sasthra Sahithya Parishad, 2006. p. 43.
14 Bhattathiripad, M.P. *Rithumathi*. Thiruvananthapuram: Maluben Publications, 2018.
15 Bhattathiripad, V.T. 'Umade Ethathyennam'. *V.T.yude Sampoorna Krithikal*. Kottayam: DC Books, 1997. p. 323.
16 Bhattathiripad, V.T. 'Namboothiri Manushyanayi Maranamenkil.' *V.T.yude Sampoorna Krithikal*. Kottayam: DC Books, 1997. p. 577.
17 Antharjanam, Lalithambika. *Lalithambika Antharjananthinte Randu Nadakangal*. Kottayam: National Book Stall, 2014.
18 Rajalakshmi, B.R. 'Punarjanmam Thedi Oru Savithrikutty.' *Granthalokam*, March, 1997. p. 36.
19 Antharjana Samajam. *Thozhil Kendrathilekku*. Thrissur: Yogakshema Press, 1948.
20 Antharjanam, Lalithambika. *Athmakathakku Oru Amukham*. Thrissur: Current Books, 1979. p. 21.
21 Ibid., p. 23.
22 Ibid., p. 22.
23 Ibid., p. 77.
24 Ibid, p. 77.
25 *Thozhil Kendrathilekku*. Scene 8, p. 82.
26 Geetha. *Penkalangal*. Thrissur: Current Books, 2010. p. 115.

27 Ushakumari, T.A., ed. *Thozhil Kendrathilekku: Natakam, Charithrarekha, Patanam*. Thrissur: Samata Publications, 2014.

Chapter 5: On the Political Stage: Women in the Leftist Revolutionary Theatre

1 Gopalakrishnan, P.K. *Purogamana Sahithrya Prasthanam: Nizhalum Velichavum*. Thrissur: Kerala Sahithya Akademi, 1987. p. 166.
2 Damodaran, K. *Pattabakki*. Kottayam: National Book Stall, 1956.
3 Thomas, C.J. *Uyarunna Yavanika*. Kottayam: National Book Stall, 2010. pp. 89–91.
4 Damodaran, *Pattabakki*, Scene 2, p. 14.
5 Ibid., Scene 3, p.20.
6 Gopalakrishnan, P.K. *Purogamana Sahithya Prasthanam*. p. 71.
7 Edasseri, Govindan Nair. *Koottukrishi*. Kozhikode: Poorna Publications, 2002.
8 Edasseri, Govindan Nair. 'Kavitha Ente Jeevithathil.' *Vishala Keralam*, Vol. 1, nd.
9 Edasseri, *Koottukrishi*, Scene 1, p. 21.
10 Ibid., Scene 2, p. 28.
11 Cherukad. *Nammalonnu*. Thiruvananthapuram: Chintha Publications, 1988.
12 Cherukad. *Jeevithapatha*. Thiruvananthapuram: Chintha Publishers, 1994. p. 505.
13 Cherukad. *Nammalonnu*. Revised version. Thrissur: Current Books, 1988.
14 Ibid., Scene 3, p. 33.

15 Ibid., Scene 7, p.81.
16 Ibid.
17 Ibid., Scene 1, p.9.
18 Ibid., Scene 7, p. 73.
19 *Lotus (India) Bulletin of the National Federation of Progressive Writers*, no. 2, 1984. p. 36.
20 Bhasi, Thoppil. *Ningalenne Communistakki* (1956). Kottayam: DC Books, 1988.
21 Unniraja, C. Preface. *Ningalenne Communistakki*. Kottayam: DC Books, 1988. p. 6.
22 Namboothiripad, EMS. *Communistaya Natakakrithu: Thoppil Bhasi Smaranika*. Unknown publisher, 2001. p. 13.
23 Sankara Pillai, G. *Malayala Nataka Sahithya Charithram*. Thrissur: Kerala Sahitya Akademi, 1980. p. 125.
24 Narayanan, Kattumadam. *Malayala Natakangaliiloode*. Palakkad: Udaya Publications, 1960. p. 72.
25 *Ningalenne Communistakki*, Scene 2, p. 31.
26 Ibid., Scene 6, p. 76.
27 Antony, P.J. *P.J. Antoniyude Sampoorna Krithikal, Vol. 1*. Kottayam: Sahithya Pravarthaka Sahakarana Sangham, 2015. pp 97–98.
28 Geenakumari, T.P.K. *Medini: Viplavavazhiyile Vanambadi*. Thrissur: Samatha, 2019. p. 54.
29 Ayamu, E.K. *Jju Nalloru Mansanakan Nokku*. Thiruvananthapuram: Chintha Publishers, 2011.
30 Ashraf, Mohammed. 'E.K. Ayamu, Jju Nalloru Mansanakan Nokku,' 2021. https://www.mlylm.in/2017/03/ek-ayamu-nilambur.html [Retrieved July 2024].

31 *Ningalenne Communistakki*, Scene 2, p. 29.
32 *Pattabakki*, Scene 12, p. 57.
33 Ibid.
34 'Ganabhushanam' was a four-year diploma course in Carnatic classical music at the Thiruvananthapuram Music Academy. The Academy, established in 1939, is currently known as the Sree Swathi Thirunal College of Music and is affiliated to the University of Kerala.
35 Nair, V. Muralidharan. *Natam Jeevithamakkiyavar*. Kottayam: DC Books, 1981. p. 101. This is the only book that contains detailed information about the life and work of Sudharma and includes a long interview with her.
36 Ibid., p. 106.
37 From the interview I conducted with Sulochana as part of the documentary, *Penmalayalam*, broadcast on Kairali TV in 2000.
38 Vijayakumari. 'Chitta Nalkiya Kalari.' *Bhashaposhini*, November, 1998.
39 Ayisha, Nilambur. *Jeevithathinte Arangu*. Thiruvananthapuram: Women's Collective, 2005. p. 43.
40 Sreekumar, K. *Oru Mukham: Janapriya Natakavediyude Miduppukal*. Kozhikode: Lipi Publications, 2005. p. 214.
41 Nair, V. Muralidharan. *Natakam Jeevithamakkiyavar*. p. 107.
42 Geenakumari, T.P.K. *Medini: Viplavavazhiyile Vanambadi*. p. 54.
43 Nair, V. Muralidharan. *Natakam Jeevithamakkiyavar*. p. 110.
44 Ayisha, Nilambur. *Jeevithathinte Arangu*. pp. 67–68.

45 Ibid., 67.
46 Mohandas, Vallikkavu. *KPACyude Charithram*. Kayamkulam: People's Arts Club, 2002. p. 116.
47 Madathil, Sajitha. *Aranginte Vakabhedangal*. Kottayam: DC Books, 2013. p. 146.

Chapter 6: A Balancing Act: The Theatre as Workplace

1 Unless otherwise stated, all first-person experiences quoted in this chapter are from my interviews and conversations with women actors. Several of the women who spoke to me requested full anonymity. In order to honour that wish, I have named the speakers only in cases where they have given consent to be named.
2 Canning, Charlotte. 'Theorizing a Feminist Theatre History.' *Theatre Journal*, Vol. 45, No. 4, 1993, pp. 529–540.
3 Lerner, Gerda. *The Majority Finds Its Past*. New York: Oxford University Press, 1979.
4 Sreekumar, K. *Oru Mukham: Janapriya Natakavediyude Midippukal*. Lipi Publications, 2005. p. 258.
5 Sulochana, KPAC. *Arangile Anubhavangal*. Thrissur: Current Books, 2007. p. 120.
6 Jose, C.L. *Natakathinte Kanappurangal*. Kottayam: DC Books, 1996.
7 Sulochana, KPAC. *Arangile Anubhavangal*. p. 120.
8 Krishnapillah, Thoppil. *Ezhayiram Ravukal–Memoir*. Thrissur: Current Books, 1996. pp. 29–30.
9 Ayisha, Nilambur. *Jeevithathinte Arangu*. Thiruvananthapuram: Women's Collective, 2005. p. 43.

10 Bhagavathar, Sebastian Kunjukunju. *Natakasmaranakal*. Thrissur: Kerala Sangeetha Nataka Akademi, 1986. p. 203.
11 Krishnapillah, Thoppil. *Ezhayiram Ravukal*, p. 29.
12 Nair, Muralidharan. *Natakam Jeevithamakkiyavar*. Kayamkulam: Kerala People's Art Class, 1981. p. 67.
13 Sulochana, KPAC. *Arangile Anubhavangal*, p. 49.

Chapter 7: Into the World of Contemporary Malayalam Theatre

1 Sankara Pillai, G. *Naandi: Natakakkalariyile Prabhashanangalum Swanubhavangalum, 1973–74*. Kottayam: National Bookstall, 1974.
2 Ibid.
3 Chandran, Civic. *Ezhupathukal Vilichappol*. Mavelikkara: Fabian Books, 2009. p. 39.
4 K.J. Baby. *Nadugaddika*. Thrissur: Current Books, 1983.
5 Joseph, Sarah. *Bhumirakshasam*. Kannur: Kairali Books, 2009.
6 Ushakumari, T.A. 'Keralathile Sthreekal.' Paper presented at the seminar 'Samatha: Utbhavavum Valarchayum.' February 11–12, 1995, Thiruvananthapuram.
7 Ibid.

Chapter 8: Of Her Own: The Emergence of Women's Theatre

1 Aston, Elaine. *Feminist Theatre Practice: A Handbook*. London: Routledge, 1999.
2 Forte, Jeanie. 'Women's Performance Art: Feminism and Postmodernism.' In *Performing Feminisms: Feminist*

Critical Theory and Theatre, edited by Sue-Ellen Case. Baltimore: Johns Hopkins University, 1990.
3 The plays staged were: *Devashilakal* (S. Sreelatha), *Rosemay Parayunnathu* (Satheesh K. Satheesh), *Fida* (Neelam Mansingh Chowdhry), *Media* (J. Sailaja), *Janus* (Divya K.), *Mandarayude Antharangam* (K.K. Subrahmanian), *Awwai* (Mangai), *God Has Changed His Name* (Avanthi Meduri), *Bhama* (Bibhash Chakraborty), *Khol do* (Maya Krishna Rao), *Himmat Ma* (Usha Ganguly), *Urumbukal Samsarikkunnathu* (C.S. Chandrika), *Ek Parikatha Aur* (Vibha Mishra), *Sundari – An Actor Prepares* (Anuradha Kapur), *The Spider's Dream* (Iganiya Kano Puga), *Beauty Parlour* (Sajitha Madathil and K.S. Sreenath).
4 Sreeja, K.V. *Ororo Kalathilum*. Kottayam: DC Books, 2004.
5 Madathil, Sajitha. *Arangile Matsygandhikal*. Thrissur: Green Books, 2018. The book won the Kerala Sahitya Akademi Award for Drama in 2019.
6 https://www.kudumbashree.org/

Scan QR code to access the Penguin Random House India website